In subsequent centuries learned men wrote and rewrote ory, compiling legends and p es linking them to the leade to Adam. The most remarka ury *Lebor Gabala (Leabhar Ga his account all but one of the en came an invasion from S ere destroyed by a plague. Ne vers had to yield to a race of monsters known as Fomhoire.

The Fir Bolg, agriculturists from Greece, were supposedly the next invaders. Then came the Tuatha De Danann, the 'tribes of the Goddess Danu', who possessed the arts of magic and were able to defeat both the Fir Bolg and the Fomhoire.

Stone Circles

These consist of upright stones arranged in a circle, and many date from the Bronze Age. There are a number of examples at Lough Gur in County Limerick. Some seem to be primitive observatories designed to measure the longest and shortest days of the year, but none is as dramatic as Stonehenge in England.

Round Cairns

The typical Bronze Age grave was a small stone-lined compartment or cist, covered by a small cairn of stones. These cairns are a familiar sight on hilltops throughout Ireland, whereas many of the larger Neolithic cairns on lower ground have had their stones re-used for walls and houses.

The last arrivals were the Sons of Mil, whose descendants were the Gaels. Although they defeated the Tuatha De Danann, the power of magic was such that the Gaels had to agree that Ireland be divided into two parts, above and below ground. The Tuatha De Danann took the lower part, becoming the underground 'fairy people', whose fairy mounds are still treated with respect by the superstitious. Written in this way the *Book of Invasions* managed to preserve in a Christian age some of the Celts' pre-Christian tradition. The Celtic gods, the Tuatha De Danann, were not banished entirely from history but allowed to continue below ground level.

The Celtic Kingdoms

Celtic Ireland was divided into a number of small kingdoms or *tuatha*, probably more than a hundred in all, each ruled by a king or *rí*. A number of these rulers were also over-kings, receiving tribute from neighbouring kings. There were also kings of provinces, but the idea of a high king, or *ard-rí* of all Ireland appears to have been a later invention. Niall of the Nine Hostages, who ruled at Tara at the beginning of the fifth century, may have been the first to claim the title of *ard-rí*. His descendants, the Ui Neill, were seldom able to press their claim to the high kingship in any material way.

Giants' Graves

The name is popularly applied to the different types of megalithic (large-stone) chambered graves of the Neolithic Age. The most interesting are the passage-graves of north central Ireland, with notable examples in the Boyne valley, at Newgrange, Knowth and Dowth. A central burial chamber is reached through a passage, and there is a covering cairn of earth or stones. Newgrange, open to the public, has a number of intricately carved stones. Gallery-graves are found throughout Ireland, and consist of a long chamber, often divided into compartments, with a longish cairn above. Some northern ones are known as court-graves or horned cairns because of a semicircular forecourt formed by upright stones. Others are known as wedge-graves, being slightly wider at the entrance, and there are many of these in the limestone Burren area of County Clare. Dolmens, in which a heavy capstone is upheld by three or more standing stones, are most common in the north. They are also known as portal-graves.

Initially Ireland was divided into the so-called 'five fifths of Ireland'. These corresponded to the present provinces of Ulster, Connacht, Munster and Leinster, except that north Leinster formed the province of Meath around Tara. Later, however, two additional units were formed on the borders of Ulster by the defeat of the Ulaid. These were Aileach and Airgialla.

Left: Tunnel at Knowth

Each king was elected from a small group of people possessing royal blood, known as the *derbfine* and comprising the male descendants of a common great-grandfather, four generations in all. Thus a king could be succeeded not only by a son or grandson, but also by an uncle or a great-nephew.

Forts and Raths

There is little visible evidence of Iron Age burials, but great numbers of the circular banks or raths that probably contained a farmhouse and kept animals from straying. Raths are seldom much more than 100 ft in diameter where there is a single bank, but in some cases there are two or three banks with intervening ditches. Where soil is thin, the rath tends to be supplanted by the cashel, which has dry-stone walls. A common feature of both raths and cashels is the souterrain or underground passage, which may have been used to store food or as a place of refuge. A similar form of dwelling is the crannog, an artificial island constructed in shallow lakes or marshes. Raths are sometimes called ring-forts, but the term is better applied to hill-forts such as Navan, County Armagh, and Tara, County Meath, where royal residences were protected by earthen ramparts. There are also substantial stone forts such as Dun Aengus in the Aran Islands, which has four defensive walls and a defensive outer perimeter of upright stones (known as *chevaux de frise*). There are also a number of promontory forts, mostly on the coast but sometimes on high ground inland, where cliffs provide natural protection on three sides. A good example is at Dunbeg, County Kerry.

Beneath the king were the nobles or *flaithi*. These were warriors and owners of cattle, and had an important role as patrons of the *aes dana*, the 'men of art', who comprised the learned classes, the poets and musicians, and the skilled craftsmen. Next came the freemen, the tillers of the soil, usually bound by contract to a nobleman. Under this contract, which could be terminated by either party, the nobleman provided protection and lent the freeman cattle to graze his land, receiving in return a rent which might consist of sacks of wheat or malt and possibly a salted pig or a young calf. There were also slaves, probably captured in war, but comparatively little is known about them and they may not have been very numerous.

Left: Navan Fort

Celtic society was essentially rural, but the members of a *tuath* or small kingdom met regularly in an assembly or *oenach* over which the king presided. This was an occasion also for games and sports. Horse racing and an equivalent of the modern Irish hurling were common, and there were board-games similar to chess or draughts. Feasts took place to the accompaniment of music and story-telling. Wine was imported from the Mediterranean and beer was brewed from Irish barley.

Standing Stones

These are single vertical stones, sometimes 20 ft high. Some mark ancient graves, some were erected comparatively recently as rubbing-stones for cattle. Two unusual round-topped stones are at Turoe, County Galway, and Castlestrange, County Roscommon. They are decorated with curving patterns of the La Tène Celtic style. Later stones bear inscriptions carved in Ogham script, a simple form of lettering consisting of strokes at right angles or diagonal to a central line. This early form of writing continued in commemorative monuments well into the Christian period.

Druids, Lawyers and Poets

In the centuries before Christianity reached Ireland the druids exercised great influence, not merely as priests but also as learned men who could judge disputes and advise kings. Their training lasted possibly a dozen years, and their traditions were passed on orally. The druids practised magic and claimed to foretell the future. They conducted public sacrifices, offering captured animals to the gods after a successful battle, and possibly there were on occasion human sacrifices. In time two other important groups emerged, the lawyers, or *brehons*, and the poets or *filidh*. Christianity meant the end of the druids, but the poets and lawyers continued to have an important place in Irish society.

The brehons were professional lawyers, and when disputes arose, it was to them that people turned as arbitrators, for there was no public enforcement of law. There was a complicated system of sureties to make certain that contracts were fulfilled or that the parties to an arbitration accepted its outcome.

Left: Standing Stone, Newgrange

The filidh were more than poets. In addition to composing and reciting poetry they were custodians of the history, mythology and genealogy of the Celts. In the Christian era they acquired much of the authority which had once belonged to the druids, and did much to preserve Irish tradition and learning at a time when the monasteries looked to the Continent for inspiration.

The earliest surviving Irish manuscripts are written in Latin, and are copies of the Gospels and the Psalms. The sagas of Celtic Ireland are found in much more recent vellum manuscripts, compiled in the twelfth century and later, although the language suggests they were copied from earlier works dating as far back as the ninth century. The most important manuscripts are the *Book of Leinster* and the *Book of the Dun Cow*, both from the twelfth century, and the *Yellow Book of Lecan* from the fourteenth century. These manuscripts contain the often-heroic tales, which the filidh handed down from generation to generation, and which are a blend of history, pagan belief and deliberate fiction.

The Coming of Christianity

The First Christians

Ireland became a Christian country in the fifth century, and St Patrick is largely credited with the conversion of the pagan Gaels and the establishment of the Church. According to tradition he landed in County Down in 432, but there were certainly Christians in Ireland before this date. Ireland had many contacts with the rest of Europe, and there was a steady trade in such commodities as wine, oil and the hides of cattle. As the Roman Empire declined, the Irish traders also became raiders, and some set up new kingdoms along the west coast of Britain. By these contacts Christian beliefs were probably brought to Ireland. It was Palladius, however, who was sent by Pope Celestine to be first bishop to the Irish 'believing in Christ'. He arrived in Ireland in 431, and until fairly recently it was believed that he died a year later, apparently in Britain, without having made much impact. Some scholars now believe that he lived and worked in Ireland for another thirty years or so, and that, because his second name was Patricius, there was some confusion among later historians between Palladius and the great Irish saint who succeeded him as bishop.

St Patrick

Much remains to be discovered about Ireland's patron saint. The traditional dates of his mission to Ireland are 432-61, but the 'two Patricks' theory suggests that he arrived in 456 and died some thirty years later. The problem is not solved by the two documents that he left behind, his *Confession* written in old age, and the much earlier *Letter to the Soldiers of Coroticus*. The saint does, however, write that he was the son of a Roman official, Calpurnius, lived in the village of Bannavem Taberniae, which may have been in Wales, and was captured at the age of sixteen by Irish raiders. For six years he was a slave in Ireland, looking after his master's sheep on a hillside commonly believed to be Slemish mountain in County Antrim. He turned to prayer, and eventually a voice told him that he should escape to a waiting ship. Patrick travelled 200 miles to the coast, where he joined a ship carrying Irish wolfhounds to the continent. Eventually he returned to Britain, where he had visions in which the people of Ireland begged him to 'come and walk again among us'.

He himself does not say where he was trained as a cleric, but a seventh-century biography suggests the monastery at Auxerre in Gaul. After many years of preparation he set sail and eventually landed on the shores of Strangford Lough. His first convert, Dichu, gave him a barn to use as a church, and the place is named Saul from the Irish for a barn, *sahall*. From this first church Patrick travelled all over Ireland, but his principal missionary work seems to have been in the north, the central lowlands and the west.

Monastic Sites
The first Christian monasteries were simple structures, built of wood or clay and wattle, and have not survived. However, a good idea of their simple layout can be gained from stone-built monasteries in the west. A good early example is the island of Skellig Michael, off the coast of County Kerry, where there are six small clochans (beehive-shaped cells), as well as oratories, stone crosses and the remains of a church. The Dingle peninsula, farther north in County Kerry, is rich in monastic sites. Among them is a perfectly preserved oratory, shaped like an upturned boat, at Gallarus, dating possibly from the eighth century.

Patrick considered himself a Roman citizen, and the church he established was Roman in character and organisation, with a number of bishops each exercising authority within his own diocese. The dioceses corresponded to the tuatha. He chose Armagh (Ard Macha, close to Emain Macha, the great hill-fort once occupied by the Gaelic kings of Ulster) as the ecclesiastical capital of Ireland, and so it remains today for both the Roman Catholic Church and the Church of Ireland. Monastic life also reached Ireland during Patrick's years as a missionary, and within a century abbots were more important than bishops and the monasteries were the main centres of both religion and learning.

Monasteries

As the Gospel spread throughout Ireland, growing numbers of people wanted to dedicate their lives to God. In a rural society there were no

Left: The Monastic Ruins of Skellig Michael, Co. Kerry

great cities where they could join together in prayer and contemplation, and so monasteries came into existence. The collapse of the Roman Empire meant that communication with the mother church was impaired, and the Celtic Church in Ireland developed its own separate character and rites, as did the churches in Scotland and Wales. Irish monasticism had an austere quality, and many monks chose to live alone or in very small groups on islands or hillsides.

Celtic Crosses

The earliest crosses were simply engraved on upright pillars, some of which bear Ogham markings. The pillars began to take the form of simple crosses, as at Carndonagh, County Donegal, dating possibly from the late sixth or early seventh century. There were also cross-slabs, flat slabs of stone delicately engraved with crosses and placed on graves. These probably date from the seventh to twelfth centuries, and there is a fine collection on display at Clonmacnois, County Offaly. The finest flowering of Celtic sculpture was the Irish High Cross, in which a circle surrounds the point of intersection. The earliest of these crosses have geometric patterns, but by the ninth century Biblical scenes are common. Among the finest High Crosses, dating to the tenth century, are the Cross of the Scriptures at Clonmacnois, the Cross of Muiredach at Monasterboice, County Louth, and the Cross of Moone, County Kildare.

The first Irish monastery to become famous was founded by St Enda on the Aran Islands at the end of the fifth century. St Finnian, who studied in Wales, founded Clonard early in the sixth century. He became known as the 'teacher of the saints of Ireland', for twelve of his pupils, sometimes known as the 'twelve apostles of Ireland', founded a number of important monasteries. They included St Columba, or Columcille (Derry and Durrow), St Ciaran (Clonmacnois, a great seat of learning overlooking the river Shannon), and St Brendan the Navigator (Clonfert).

The early Irish monasteries were groups of simple buildings, quite unlike the great monasteries of Europe. They included a church, a refectory, the monks' cells, schools, a library and a workshop. The

Left: The Ardboe Cross, Co. Tyrone

monasteries were usually made of wood or wattle, with thatched roofs, but stone was used in the barren west and this ultimately became the practice throughout the island.

The monks shaved their hair at the front of their heads and let it grow long at the back, a style of tonsure that contrasted with the continental practice of shaving the crown of the head. More important than the divergence over tonsure was the Celtic Church's adherence to a traditional method of dating Easter, while the Roman Church accepted a new method devised by Victorius of Aquitaine in 457. Not until 716 did the Columban monasteries conform to Roman practice, and thereafter Armagh rather than the Columban monastery on the Scottish island of Iona was the supreme centre of the Irish Church.

Illuminated Manuscripts
Surviving manuscripts are illustrated in the same distinctive Celtic style as the High Crosses and the metalwork. The finest of the illuminated gospel books, laboriously compiled by monks, are the seventh century Book of Durrow and the eighth-century Book of Kells, both in the library of Trinity College, Dublin.

St Columcille, whose name meant 'dove of the Church', was the most remarkable of the monastic leaders. The event which, it is commonly believed, changed his life came after he had founded religious houses at Derry and Durrow. While staying with St Finnian of Moville he secretly copied a gospel text belonging to his host.

Finnian became angry and claimed the copy, and King Diarmaid ruled 'To every cow her calf, to every book its copy'. Columcille rejected the finding, and there followed a battle in which many were killed. It is said that, as a penance, he chose exile in a foreign land where he could win for Christianity as many souls as had died in the battle. Columcille sailed to Iona in 563, and for three centuries the monastery he founded there was the most renowned in the Celtic fringes of Britain.

Ireland is sometimes called the land of saints and scholars, and the name derives from this golden age of the Irish Church, when great numbers of 'pilgrims for Christ' followed Columcille's example and

Left: Celtic style lettering.

spread with missionary fervour throughout Britain and Western Europe. For many it was an act of penitence, but there was also a firm desire to convert the pagan hordes which had destroyed the Roman Empire. One ninth-century author wrote of an Irish nation 'with whom the custom of travelling into foreign parts has now become almost second nature'.

St Columbanus was the most famous Irish monk to work on the continent, and in propagating Celtic ideas about confession of sins and penance he had more influence on the Church as a whole than Columcille. In 590 Columbanus sailed for France from Bangor, where he had studied under the strict and scholarly St Comgall, and before he died in 615 founded monasteries in France, Germany and Italy. The most renowned were at Luxeuil and Bobbio.

The European Monasteries
The twelfth century saw the arrival of Cistercian monks from the continent, soon to be followed by Augustinians, Benedictines, Franciscans and Dominicans. The older Irish foundations soon yielded to the newcomers, whose better ordered lives were reflected in the well planned architecture of their monasteries. Although succeeding centuries brought ravages and neglect, the ruins of these medieval buildings are among Ireland's most impressive monuments. There are good examples of Cistercian monasteries at Mellifont, County Louth, Jerpoint, County Kilkenny and Inch, County Down. The twelfth and thirteenth centuries also saw the building of many cathedrals. Some are still in use, with substantial re-building, as at Kilkenny, Limerick and Clonfert, County Galway. Others, such as Cormac's Cathedral at Cashel, County Tipperary, are in ruins.

The Vikings

Although the Irish often fought among themselves during the early centuries of Christianity, it was not until the end of the eighth century that the island was menaced by a new set of invaders. These were the Vikings, and their first recorded attack was on the island of Lambay, off the east coast, where St Columcille had founded a monastery. In the

Left: Detail from 'The Weepers', Jerpoint Abbey

Above: Memorial to Brian Boru at the Church of Ireland Cathedral, Armagh

same year, 795, the Scandinavian warriors plundered Iona. There were other raids on Iona, and after sixty-eight monks had been murdered in 806, the survivors fled to Ireland and established a new monastery at Kells, in Meath. All round the Irish coast monasteries fell to the helmeted invaders whose longships appeared suddenly from the sea. The shallow draught of the vessels meant that the Vikings could sail up rivers like the Shannon and the Bann. Thorgest or Turgesius had fleets on Lough Ree and Lough Neagh, and he drove out the abbot of Armagh. In 845 Thorgest was captured and killed by Malachy, the King of Meath, and thereafter the Irish began to have some success in battle.

The Vikings were not only interested in plunder, but also in trade and settling new lands less crowded than the narrow fjord valleys of their Norwegian homeland. In 841 they built a stockaded settlement or *longphort* on the river Liffey, and this was to become the city of Dublin. Other major Irish towns, such as Wicklow, Wexford, Waterford, Cork and

Limerick, were also founded by the Vikings. The Irish economy expanded, and silver coins were minted for the first time in Dublin. The ports became centres of power and influence, and the east coast gradually became more important than inland centres such as Tara and Armagh.

The dominant dynasties in ninth-century Ireland were the Ui Neill at Tara and the Eoganachta at Cashel. However, a new force arose in Munster, the Dal Cais, and in 964 their King Mahon seized the throne of Cashel. Mahon's younger brother, Brian Boru, succeeded him in 976 and became so powerful that in 1002 the leader of the Ui Neill yielded the high kingship to him without fighting. In 1014 Brian defeated an alliance of Dublin Norsemen under Sigurd, Earl of Orkney, and Leinstermen under Mael Morda at the battle of Clontarf. He died at the moment of victory, slain by a fleeing Norseman who entered his unguarded tent. Henceforth the role of the Norsemen in Ireland was largely a peaceful one. Most of them had given up pagan beliefs, and they intermarried with the Irish and concentrated on developing trade. They became known as Ostmen (men of the east), and severed their ties with Scandinavia.

Brian Boru
Born c. 940, succeeded his brother Mahon or Mathgamain as king of the Dal Cais in County Clare in 976. He fought successfully against the Norsemen and their Irish allies, and slew his brother's killer in 978. By 984 Brian controlled southern Ireland with the help of a large fleet on the river Shannon. In 997 he and Malachy, the high king at Tara, agreed to divide the island between them, but in 1002 Brian forced Malachy to submit to him. Brian described himself as Emperor of the Irish, and in comparative peace he helped to rebuild churches and restore libraries. His greatest victory was in 1014 at Clontarf, where he defeated an alliance of Norsemen and Leinstermen, but the aged high king was slain by the axe of Broder, a fleeing Norseman.

Reform of the Church

Not surprisingly the period of disruption caused the Church's moral standards to fall. In many monasteries the abbot was a layman, there was no effective organisation of dioceses, and the Church's teaching was often ignored in such matters as marriage, divorce and baptism.

However, a reform movement was already underway on the continent, and its influence spread to Ireland. At first the Celtic Church tried to hold on to its traditional separatism, resisting the claims of the Norman archbishops of Canterbury to exercise jurisdiction over the whole of Britain and Ireland. It was the Ostmen who first accepted church government from England, and for a period the bishops of Dublin were consecrated by the Archbishop of Canterbury. In 1111 a synod was held at Rathbresail near Cashel, and Ireland was divided into twenty-four dioceses, with archbishops at Armagh and Cashel.

Round Towers

The earliest stone churches were simple buildings, probably very similar in shape to their wooden predecessors. Many were stone-roofed, and an interesting feature is the stone arch which supports the steeply pitched roof and at the same time creates an attic room above the main body of the church, which also has an arched ceiling. Good examples are St Kevin's Kitchen at Glendalough, County Wicklow, and Cormac's Chapel at Cashel, County Tipperary. More famous, however, are the tall Round Towers found at many monastic sites. These were built during the tenth to twelfth centuries after the Viking invasions, and were places of refuge as well as watch towers and belfries. The entrance is well above ground level, and movable ladders allowed the monks to retreat to higher floors of the tapering towers, some well over 100 ft high. In some cases only the stump of the original tower remains, but there are well preserved examples at Ardmore, County Waterford, and Antrim town.

St Malachy was the greatest of the Irish reformers. Born in Armagh in 1094 he became Archbishop of Armagh in 1132. In 1137 he retired to Bangor, but two years later was sent to Rome by his successor at Armagh. His mission was to acquire for the archbishops of Armagh and Cashel the *pallia* or lamb's wool collars which would signify the Pope's recognition of their position and of the reforms that they had carried out. On his way he stayed with St Bernard, the head of the Cistercian order, at Clairvaux and was so impressed that he sent a number of monks to be trained there. The first Cistercian foundation in Ireland was established at

Left: Round Tower at Narrow Water

Mellifont in 1142, and there were eventually thirty-nine Cistercian houses on the island. Meanwhile Pope Innocent II had told Malachy that a national synod must request the pallia, and the saint died in 1148 on a second journey to Rome. It was the Synod of Kells in 1152 which gave the Irish Church the shape it still retains. Dublin and Tuam joined Armagh and Cashel as archbishoprics, and thirty-six dioceses were established. The effect was to end the Ostmen's allegiance to Canterbury, and the Archbishop of Armagh was recognised as Primate of All Ireland.

Celtic Metalwork

The intricate but dignified design of the High Crosses was paralleled in the metalwork of the period, of which the best examples are in the National Museum in Dublin. The Ardagh Chalice is made of silver and decorated with glass studs and delicate gold filigree. It belongs to the eighth century, as does the Tara Brooch, which consists of a decorated silver ring with an ornamented pin. Another treasure is the Moylough Belt Reliquary, a bronze shrine probably made to hold a saint's belt. The museum has a number of crosiers from the eleventh and twelfth centuries, of which the best preserved is the Lismore Crosier. Also from the twelfth century are the Shrine of Saint Patrick's Bell and the glorious Cross of Cong, a shrine made to hold a fragment of the True Cross. It is made of oak, encased in silver and copper and decorated in gold and gilt bronze, with a large quartz crystal at the centre.

Kings with Opposition

With the death of Brian Boru in 1014 Ireland again became an island of conflicting dynasties, with the high kingship as the prize. The term *rí con fresabra* or 'king with opposition' was used for those who claimed the high kingship but were unable to enforce acceptance by all the provinces. In 1162 Murtough MacLochlainn was acknowledged high king, but his success was short-lived. In 1166 he blinded the captive King of Ulidia, contrary to the guarantees under which the latter had surrendered, and was killed in the rebellion which followed this brutality. Rory O'Connor became high king, and his ally Tiernan O'Rourke of Brefni seized the chance to settle an old score with Murtough's ally, Dermot MacMurrough, who had once carried off his wife Dervorgilla. However, when Tiernan invaded Leinster, Dermot fled to England in search of allies. Although the Gaelic kingdoms had been moving gradually towards a strong central monarchy, the process was incomplete and the Irish were not well enough organised to repel the Anglo-Norman invasion which followed Dermot's flight.

The Normans in Ireland

Strongbow

A century had passed since William the Conqueror's defeat of Harold at the battle of Hastings. England was a Norman kingdom, and the powerful Norman barons had tamed the lowlands of Scotland and Wales. They were the most efficient warriors in Europe, and matched their military successes with an administrative skill which ensured the profitability of their ventures. When Dermot MacMurrough landed in Bristol he was advised to seek out Henry II, who was then in his French duchy of Aquitaine. Henry accepted Dermot's allegiance, and in return gave him permission to recruit among his subjects for an Irish expedition. It was in the Welsh borders, where the Normans fought a continuing battle with the native Welsh, that Dermot struck a bargain with the Anglo-Norman warrior known as Strongbow. His full name was Richard FitzGilbert de Clare, Earl of Pembroke, and he agreed to restore Dermot to the kingship of Leinster in return for marriage to Dermot's eldest daughter Aoife and the right to succeed him as king.

Dermot returned to Ireland in 1167 with a small force of Normans, Welsh and Flemings, but it was 1169 before the first major contingent of Normans landed at Bannow Bay in County Wexford. A force of Norsemen from the town of Wexford challenged them, but soon yielded to the disciplined foot soldiers, archers with deadly crossbows and knights in chain mail. Dermot next wrote to Strongbow, pressing him to come to Ireland, and in 1170 an advance force under Raymond Le Gros landed at Baginbun headland near Bannow. They threw up ramparts just in time to withstand an attack from a much larger force of Norsemen from Waterford and Irish, then routed their opponents by driving cattle against them. Seventy leading townsmen from Waterford were taken prisoner, and the Normans broke their limbs and threw them off the nearby cliffs. It was an important victory, and an old couplet records:

> *At the creeke of Baginbunne*
> *Ireland was lost and wonne.*

A few weeks later Strongbow arrived with more than a thousand troops, seized Waterford and married Aoife MacMurrough in its cathedral. In September 1170 he captured Dublin when two young knights grew impatient of negotiations with the Ostmen and launched a surprise attack. When Dermot died in the following spring Strongbow became King of Leinster. However, the Normans still faced opposition. First the deposed Norse earl, Asgall, returned with a large fleet recruited in the Scottish Hebrides and the Isle of Man. Then, after Asgall had been defeated and beheaded, the high king Rory O'Connor besieged Dublin. After two months the hungry Normans again made a surprise sortie, routing the high king's army and capturing its ample stocks of food. The Normans had again demonstrated their military superiority, and there was no further danger that they would be driven out of Ireland.

The Norman Conquest

It was at this point that Henry II, fearful that Strongbow would set up an independent kingdom, chose to establish himself as overlord of Ireland. As early as 1155 Henry had sought and won the approval of Pope Adrian IV for an invasion of Ireland, and the papal bull *Laudabiliter* recognised him as lord of Ireland and commissioned him to carry out religious reforms. He now had the additional object of providing a lordship, possibly a separate kingdom, to which his infant son John might succeed. The king landed at Waterford in October 1171 with a large army. Strongbow was the first to submit to him, and in return Henry granted him the kingdom of Leinster. Dermot McCarthy, King of Desmond (south Munster), was the first Irish king to submit, offering tribute to his Norman overlord, and others quickly followed. The Irish bishops met at Lismore and swore their loyalty. Only the high king, Rory O'Connor, and the northern kings remained aloof.

In April 1172 Henry ended his only visit to Ireland. If the Irish chiefs hoped that they had made only a token submission, they were mistaken. Henry's last act was to appoint a justiciar or viceroy, Hugh de Lacy, to whom he granted the kingdom of Meath in a demonstration of his supreme powers as overlord. He also annexed the cities of Dublin, Wexford, Waterford, Cork and Limerick as crown demesnes, and left garrisons in all of them. The Norman barons, intent on further conquest, quickly began to extend their territories by driving out the Irish chiefs. A spirited resistance eventually led to the Treaty of Windsor in 1175. Henry recognised Rory O'Connor as king of Connacht in return for annual tribute, and also as high king of those areas which remained in Irish

hands. However, Henry soon violated the treaty by granting new lands to his barons, and Norman castles continued to multiply. Indeed by the middle of the thirteenth century the Normans had gained control of most of Ireland. Only the northern kingdoms of Tir Eoghain and Tir Conaill withstood the conquest, while Connacht was only sparsely settled.

Castles

The first Norman fortifications were wooden towers built on artificial mounds or mottes, with an enclosure or bailey at the foot of the mound. Many of these mounds remain, as at Granard, County Longford, but the motte-and-bailey soon gave way to substantial stone castles. The main period for castle building lasted from the late twelfth to the early fourteenth century. The typical castle had a central tower or keep, which might or might not be embodied in the surrounding walls. The keep might be rectangular, circular or (a contrast to Norman castles elsewhere) rectangular with a circular tower at each corner. Good examples of the rectangular keep are Carrickfergus Castle, County Antrim, where the keep forms part of the wall, and Trim Castle, County Meath, where it does not. Nenagh Castle, County Tipperary, has a fine round keep. The best preserved towered keep is at Ferns, County Wexford. Some Norman castles, including those at Dublin, Kilkenny and Limerick, were built without keeps. The later keepless castles tend to have substantial towers protruding outwards from the walls, as well as pairs of towers protecting the main entrance. There is an excellent example at Roscommon.

Life under the Normans

The Normans introduced to Ireland the feudal system of government and land tenure which already existed in England and much of Europe. All land belonged to the king, who granted it to others in return for homage and specified dues or services. In return for Leinster Strongbow had to provide a hundred knights whenever the king requested them. Hugh de Lacy was granted Meath in return for fifty knights. More than four hundred knights were called for under all the land grants or fiefs, but in many cases an equivalent sum of money known as scutage was accepted.

Left: Dunguire Castle

Each major landlord divided his holding among lesser lords, who in turn had sub-tenants. A tenant's land was inherited by his eldest son, who paid a sum in recognition of the landlord's original right to distribute the land as he pleased. If there were no son, the land was divided equally between any daughters, a practice which seriously weakened some of the Norman holdings.

Tower Houses

After more than a hundred years, during which there was little major building, there was a revival in the middle of the fifteenth century. Typical of the following 150 years, and both numerous and widespread, is the tower house. This fortified residence is usually rectangular in shape, rising to crenellated parapets, sometimes with one or more projecting turrets. Tower houses are sometimes known as '£10 castles', for Henry VI introduced a subsidy in 1429 to encourage the defence of the Pale. There are good examples at Clara, County Kilkenny, and Roodstown, County Louth. Both have a 'murder-hole' over the entrance, allowing defenders above to assail unwelcome visitors. A few towers are circular, including Reginald's Tower in Waterford, which now houses a museum. Tower houses normally had a fortified enclosure or bawn attached to them.

The Normans gave Ireland its first effective central government. The justiciar, later known as the king's lieutenant, was head of the civil administration, commander of the king's army and chief judge. The justiciar was assisted by a council, and this came to consist largely of the most important officials in the administration. He also convened a parliament from time to time. This at first consisted of his council, the major feudal lords, bishops and abbots. Towards the end of the thirteenth century representatives of the counties and towns were summoned to parliament, where they formed a lower house or commons. Taxation was the principal concern of parliament but legislation was passed to deal with particular problems rather than major questions, since English legislation generally applied to Ireland.

A major Norman contribution was the creation of towns. Hitherto there had only been the Viking settlements around the coast and monastic

Left: Barrow Castle

centres like Clonmacnois and Armagh. Now towns developed around castles and manors. Mills, workshops and monasteries were built, and trade developed. Towns like Kilkenny, Kildare, Athlone and, on the coast, Galway and Drogheda owe their origin to the Normans. The towns enjoyed an increasing number of privileges and tended to be loyal to the English king rather than to the Norman lords or the Irish kings.

Gaelic Resistance

It has been said that the tragedy of the Norman invasion was not the conquest of Ireland but the half-conquest. Had the conquest been completed, as in England, a new nation would have emerged. Instead there was a shifting frontier between native Irish and Norman invader, and 'the Irish question' began to make its mark on English political life.

There were several reasons why the conquest slowed to a halt. The feudal barons weakened themselves in internal struggles. Royal justice proved difficult to enforce, as successive English kings were distracted by wars against Wales, Scotland and France. Eventually, too, the Irish kings learned to fight back, and in 1270 Aedh O'Connor, the king of Connacht, defeated an Anglo-Irish army led by the justiciar Ralph d'Ufford and Walter de Burgo. An important factor in the Irish victory at Athankip was the gallowglasses, professional foot soldiers of Norse-Scottish stock who wore helmets and mail and wielded heavy axes. The first gallowglasses (in Irish *gall oglaigh*, foreign warriors) had arrived in Tir Conaill from the western islands and highlands of Scotland a few years before, and they were to become the spearhead of Gaelic resistance for the next 300 years.

Robert and Edward Bruce

In 1314 Robert Bruce, King of Scotland, won a major victory over an English army at Bannockburn. Edward II had drawn on Ireland for soldiers and supplies, and Robert Bruce saw in an Irish invasion a chance to weaken the English and find a kingdom for his brother Edward. It was Edward Bruce who landed at Larne in 1315 with 6,000 men. He was joined by a number of Irish chiefs, and he soon defeated the Earl of Ulster at Connor. Within a year he was crowned king of Ireland near Dundalk, and his successes encouraged risings in different parts of the island. There was no real unity of purpose, however, and at Athenry an Irish army under Felim O'Connor was heavily defeated by William de Burgo, who thus restored his family's fortunes in Connacht.

Edward Bruce took Carrickfergus after a long siege, and early in 1317 he was joined by his brother Robert with a large army. They marched south, burning and plundering, but retreated again to Ulster. Robert returned to Scotland, and gradually the new lord lieutenant, Roger Mortimer, began to restore peace in other parts of Ireland. Pope John XXII excommunicated Edward and his supporters. In May 1318 an Irish army under Murtough O'Brien defeated a Norman force under Richard de Clare at Dysert O'Dea, and ensured Irish supremacy in Thomond (north Munster). Edward, however, was defeated and killed at Faughart, near Dundalk, five months later when he challenged a superior colonial army under John de Bermingham. Nonetheless the Bruces had succeeded in disrupting the Anglo-Norman colony in Ireland, and it never regained its earlier authority. The Irish for their part were not sorry to see the end of a man whose ravages had brought widespread famine.

The Decline of the Colony

As early as 1297 the Irish parliament in Dublin passed legislation penalising 'degenerate Englishmen' who wore their hair in the flowing Irish style and requiring colonists to provide for the defence of their lands. After the Bruce invasion the government was increasingly troubled by the growing military strength of the Gaelic rulers and by the willingness of Norman lords to ally themselves with them and to engage in wars which could only weaken the king's grip on Ireland. Many Normans were absentee landlords, more interested in their holdings in England or in waging war in France. Some colonists became 'more Irish than the Irish', while others left the island.

In 1361 Edward III appointed his son, Lionel of Clarence, as king's lieutenant in Ireland, and in February 1366 the latter held a parliament at Kilkenny. It produced the most notorious Irish legislation of the Middle Ages. The Statutes of Kilkenny were both recognition that the Norman conquest must remain incomplete and an attempt to ensure that at least part of Ireland remained English in character and loyal to the king. Under this legislation there could be no alliance between English and Irish, whether by marriage, concubinage, fostering of children or *gossipred* (sponsoring another's child at baptism). The colonists were required to speak English, have English names, and keep to English customs and dress. They were not allowed to have Irish minstrels 'since they spy out their secrets'. They could not sell horses or armour to the Irish, or victuals in time of war. The Irish could not be admitted to cathedrals, or to any ecclesiastical benefice or religious house among the English. The Irish living among the English were required to speak English even among themselves. Much of the legislation was concerned with defence, and the colonists were urged to practise archery and the use of lances rather than hurling and other ball games. At best Lionel hoped to hold one-third of the island for the king, leaving the rest to the Gaelic rulers and the 'degenerate English' but after he left Ireland in November 1366 the influence of the colony continued to decline, and eventually the government in Dublin paid so-called 'black rents' to some Irish rulers not to attack. Richard II, who brought large armies to Ireland in 1394 and 1399, was no more successful in delivering the colonists from 'Irish enemies and English rebels'.

The Great Earls

For more than a century there was a resurgence of Gaelic life and culture. The English colony, known as the Pale, dwindled in size. The Irish chiefs were virtually independent, and governed according to brehon laws rather than the statutes of Dublin. There was a great revival in Gaelic learning, and many important manuscripts date from the fourteenth and fifteenth centuries.

Three powerful Anglo-Irish lordships came to dominate the island. These were the earldoms of Ormond (Tipperary and Kilkenny), held by the Butler family, and Desmond (Cork, Kerry and Limerick) and Kildare, both held by branches of the Fitzgerald family. The Geraldines, as they were known, became 'more Irish than the Irish', and the third Earl of Desmond was himself a noted writer of Irish verse. The Butlers retained closer ties with England, but the powerful fourth Earl of Ormond made his seat at Kilkenny an important centre of Anglo-Irish culture and was a strong advocate of 'home rule'.

The most famous Anglo-Irish leader was the eighth Earl of Kildare, Garret More, known as the 'Great Earl'. Born 1456, he was elected justiciar by the council of Ireland in 1477 on his father's death, and resisted English attempts to unseat him until 1494. Henry VII sent over Sir Edward Poynings as viceroy to reduce the lordship of Ireland to 'whole and perfect obedience'. Poynings' Parliament, as it is known, met at Drogheda in 1494, and accused Garret More of treason, for supporting the claims of pretender-to-the-throne Lambert Simnel. An Act known as Poynings' Law required that the Irish parliament should only meet with the king's approval and pass only legislation agreed by the king and his council. Garret More was imprisoned in the Tower of London, but Henry restored him as deputy soon afterwards, saying 'Since all Ireland cannot rule this man, this man must rule all Ireland'. Virtually an uncrowned king until his death in 1513, Garret More had encouraged a flowering of Gaelic culture and a growing sense of common identity between the traditional Irish chiefs and Old English rulers like himself. His son Garret Oge continued the Kildare dominance. In 1534 Garret Oge was summoned to London, and he left his son Thomas, Lord Offaly, as deputy. The hot-headed 'Silken Thomas' believed an untrue report that his father had been beheaded, and rode to Dublin to tell the council that he was no longer the king's deputy but his foe.

The Tudor Conquest

Henry VIII

The rebellion of Silken Thomas provided the English king, Henry VIII, an opportunity to destroy the Geraldine supremacy and extend his authority over the whole island. Whether he planned so complete a conquest as occurred is uncertain, but there were good defensive reasons for subduing Ireland, for it might have been used as a base for Spanish aggression. The English also looked on the neighbouring island as suitable for commercial exploitation, and Irish 'plantations' were the forerunners of American colonies.

In October 1534 Sir William Skeffington landed with a large army and installed himself as deputy. Silken Thomas's stronghold at Maynooth was captured the following March, and those who surrendered were executed for 'the dread and example of others'. The 'pardon of Maynooth', as it was called, proved to be a portent of new levels of violence in Ireland. Silken Thomas himself surrendered in August, and was executed in London in 1537 with five Geraldine uncles. The ninth Earl had also died, and of the house of Kildare, only Thomas's ten-year-old half-brother Gerald remained. Henceforth, for almost four centuries, there would always be an Englishman at the head of the Irish government.

The Gaelic and Old English lords still offered some resistance, however, and a Geraldine league was formed to ensure the survival of the young heir, who was sent to safety in Italy. Henry opted for a peaceful policy of 'surrender and regrant', by which the Gaelic and Old English lords pledged allegiance to him and gave up their lands to the crown, receiving them back as feudal grants. The 'Irish enemies' and 'English rebels' had to accept English laws, language and customs, and to recognise Henry rather than the Pope as 'the only Supreme Head on Earth of the whole Church of Ireland'.

The Reformation

Silken Thomas's followers had murdered John Alen, Archbishop of Dublin, in 1534. In 1536 he was succeeded by George Browne, to whom Henry VIII entrusted the task of imposing reform on a church little touched by the intellectual ferment of the Protestant Reformation. A 'Reformation parliament' met under the new deputy, Lord Grey, and passed acts confirming Henry's supremacy, making it treason to describe the king as a heretic, and outlawing anyone who supported the Pope as head of the Church. Despite opposition from the bishops an act was passed to dissolve the abbeys of Ireland. Outside the Pale many monasteries survived, although their lands had been granted to Gaelic and Old English lords. Where monasteries did disappear, they left a gap in social and educational activities which the Established Church seldom filled.

Edward VI was nine years old when he became king in 1547, and power rested with his uncle and 'Protector', the Duke of Somerset. An attempt was made to impose the use of the English *Book of Common Prayer*, but there was widespread resistance to changes in the form of the Mass, and the government was not strong enough to support Archbishop Browne in punitive measures. By this time Henry VIII's peaceful policies had been supplanted by a more aggressive attitude towards the Gaelic rulers, and the 'English land' was being extended by forfeiture of land accompanied by the establishment of new military garrisons.

When Mary Tudor came to the throne in 1553 an attempt was made to reduce the military commitment. Land which had been confiscated from the O'Mores and O'Connors in counties Laois and Offaly was allocated for plantation by settlers from England or from the Pale, and they were renamed Queen's County and King's County. Mary was a devout Catholic and acknowledged the supremacy of the Pope, but she continued to nominate the Irish bishops and made no attempt to restore the monasteries.

Elizabethan Ireland

Queen Mary died in 1558 and was succeeded by her half-sister, Elizabeth, who immediately set about restoring Protestant dominance. An Irish parliament met briefly in 1560, and passed an Act of Supremacy, confirming Elizabeth as head of the Irish church and requiring holders of various offices in Church and State to swear an oath accepting her as such. An Act of Uniformity imposed the new *Book of Common Prayer* on all clergy, although few people in Ireland understood the English language in which it was written, and church attendance was made compulsory. Although both acts were implemented with discretion, so that there was no substantial religious persecution, resistance to the Protestant religion became a factor in the hostility of Irish and Old English rulers to the Tudor regime.

Ulster was to prove the most difficult province to subdue, but Elizabeth also faced resistance in other parts of the island. In 1569 James Fitzmaurice Fitzgerald, the able cousin of the fifteenth Earl of Desmond, led an unsuccessful rebellion after an English adventurer called Sir Peter Carew had laid claim to estates belonging to the Fitzgeralds and the Butlers. James then escaped to the continent, and in 1579 returned with a small force of Italians and Spaniards, together with a papal nuncio, to engage in 'a war for the Catholic religion'. The second Desmond rebellion was also defeated, but this time Munster was laid waste and much of the province was declared forfeit so that it could be planted by English settlers.

Hugh O'Neill

Born 1550, son of Matthew O'Neill, Baron of Dungannon. Matthew's claim to be the legitimate eldest son of the ruling Conn O'Neill, first Earl of Tyrone, was disputed by the younger son Shane, who later had Matthew murdered. After Conn's death in 1559 Hugh was taken to England by Queen Elizabeth's lord deputy, Sir Henry Sidney, and educated as an English nobleman. He returned in 1567, and served the queen so loyally that in 1585 the Irish parliament granted him the earldom of Tyrone. Yet his loyalty became suspect when he spared shipwrecked Spaniards who had survived the Armada's defeat in 1588, and when in 1590 he slew an informer according to Gaelic rather than Tudor law. Eventually he was forced to defend the Gaelic world he loved against English encroachment, and he came close to uniting the Irish in victory. He took the imposing title of 'The O'Neill' in 1593, and in 1595 went to war. He won a major victory at the Yellow Ford on the river Blackwater in 1598, but was heavily defeated at Kinsale, far from his native Ulster, in 1601. He surrendered in 1603, and in 1607 he and many other Ulster chiefs chose to exile themselves in Europe. He died in Rome in 1616.

When the Spanish Armada was routed in 1588, the surviving galleons sought shelter off the west coast of Ireland, where most were driven ashore or sank in bad weather. Those Spaniards who reached dry ground were quickly executed, except in Ulster, which remained largely untouched by Tudor conquest and the attempt to anglicise Ireland. It had

Above: Kinsale, where O'Neill suffered defeat to the English

become clear, however, that Ulster would have to fight to retain its independence. Hugh O'Neill, Earl of Tyrone, took up the challenge, and was to prove a formidable statesman and soldier. His principal ally was Red Hugh O'Donnell, the ruler of Tyrconnell, whose bitter hatred of the English stemmed from his youthful imprisonment in Dublin as a hostage.

Fighting broke out in 1594, but not until 1598 did O'Neill show his potential strength as a national leader by defeating Sir Henry Bagenal at the Battle of the Yellow Ford in Armagh. In Munster a general uprising swept away the English plantation. Elsewhere a number of Irish rulers rebelled. In 1599 the Earl of Essex arrived in Ireland with a large army, but O'Neill outmanoeuvred him, and Lord Mountjoy assumed command in the following year. Mountjoy set about garrisoning the country, and used his troops to destroy O'Neill's food supplies and communications. O'Neill sought help from Spain, but the Spanish army landed in 1601 at Kinsale in the south. O'Neill and O'Donnell marched to join the invaders, but were heavily defeated in unfamiliar country. O'Donnell sailed to Spain, where he died soon afterwards, but O'Neill continued the war. One by one the Gaelic rulers yielded, and in 1603 O'Neill himself signed the Treaty of Mellifont. Queen Elizabeth had died a few days before his surrender, and James I did not impose a harsh settlement. However, there was no doubt that the Tudor conquest was now complete and that the old Gaelic society was doomed.

Ireland under the Stuarts

The Plantation of Ulster

The Treaty of Mellifont was a generous settlement, and the great Ulster chiefs were restored to their lands. Nevertheless they were now landlords rather than kings and the English garrisons were a constant reminder that they could fall victim to any reversal of the government's conciliatory policy. In 1607 O'Neill, Rory O'Donnell, brother of Red Hugh, and more than ninety other Ulster chiefs sailed into voluntary exile on the continent. This 'flight of the earls' gave the government an opportunity to declare their lands forfeit to the crown. In all the lord deputy, Sir Arthur Chichester, confiscated six of the nine Ulster counties. These were Donegal, Fermanagh, Cavan, Armagh, Tyrone and Coleraine, the last of these being renamed Londonderry.

The Articles of Plantation were published in May 1609, and provided for the settlement of half a million acres of 'profitable' land. The task was largely entrusted to 'undertakers', who were to bring in English and Scottish settlers, set up villages and towns, build fortified enclosures or 'bawns' and generally provide for the defence of their lands. Land was also granted to 'servitors', men who had already served the crown in Ireland, but they were allowed to take Irish tenants as well as English and Scottish planters. Finally in each county a small proportion of land was allocated to Irish landlords, who were required to adopt English methods of husbandry.

The Plantation profoundly altered the Ulster landscape, and gave the province a population markedly different from other parts of Ireland. The most substantial single enterprise was the planting of Londonderry, which was undertaken by a group of London guilds. Yet there, as in many other parts of Ulster, the undertakers were unable to attract enough tenants from England and Scotland. Consequently they accepted Irish tenants, and Chichester's hopes of establishing clearly defined areas of 'civil men well affected in religion' were thwarted. Protestant settlement was actually most successful in the two eastern counties of Antrim and Down, where two private adventurers from Scotland, Hugh Montgomery and James Hamilton, contrived to acquire a good deal of land close to Belfast. Large numbers of immigrants from the nearby Scottish lowlands took up holdings in south Antrim and north Down, and the native Irish were largely dispossessed.

The new settlers quickly built towns, which were designed in orderly patterns and contrasted with the untidy cluster of huts which the native Irish occupied. The towns were protected by walls or earthen banks, and the planters armed themselves against possible attacks by the resentful Irish. The towns were given royal charters, and governed by burgesses chosen from leading Protestants who took the oath of supremacy acknowledging the king as head of the Irish Church. The burgesses elected two members of parliament to represent the town, and in this way the government quickly assured itself of a Protestant majority in parliament. The success of the Ulster plantation was sufficient to persuade the government to attempt similar ventures in other parts of Ireland, and Irish landholders were dispossessed in parts of Longford, Leitrim, Offaly, Wexford, Wicklow and Carlow.

The Stuart Administration

In 1613 Sir Arthur Chichester summoned a parliament in Dublin. The presence of the Church of Ireland bishops ensured a Protestant majority of 24 to 12 in the upper house, and the creation of new boroughs produced a majority of 132 to 10 in the commons. The numbers of native Irish had been reduced by the 'flight of the earls', and most of the Catholics were Old English. They were prepared to accept such measures as the attainting of O'Neill and O'Donnell, the recognition of the king's title and provision for road maintenance, but they were rightly fearful of anti-Catholic legislation. The government planned measures to prevent the common practice of sending Irish boys to the continent for their education, to curb Jesuits and to make the more severe legislation of England applicable to Ireland. The Old English complained about the new boroughs, opposed unsuccessfully the government nominee for the speakership of the commons and finally withdrew from both houses. The king, unwilling to let this breach continue, reduced the boroughs' representation. There was still a Protestant majority, but the government did not pursue its penal measures.

Parliament was dissolved in 1615, and it was 1634 before another was convened. Chichester was recalled to England in 1615, but his successors under James I continued his policies of tolerant administration. The Oath of Supremacy kept the Old English out of office, but the recusancy fines (for not attending the state church) were generally ignored. However, the Catholics could never be sure that conditions

Above: Charles Fort, Co. Cork

would not deteriorate, and outside the government there was a hardening of puritanical Protestant feeling. This was reflected in the 104 articles of religion issued by the first convocation of the whole Church of Ireland in 1615, which were much more Calvinistic than the Thirty-nine Articles of the Church of England. The Catholics were also disturbed by the legal trickery which allowed the plantations to be extended outside Ulster.

The Plantations

The Tudor and Stuart periods brought the construction of more comfortable residences, with fewer storeys and more windows, yet better designed for defence than their English counterparts. They were still known as castles, and usually had a gabled rectangular block with square towers at each corner. A good example is at Monkstown, County Cork. It was common to add a house to an earlier tower, as at Loughmoe, County Tipperary. In Donegal Castle a fine Jacobean wing with many gables has been grafted on to a much renovated tower built by the O'Donnells.

Under the terms of the Ulster Plantation, English and Scottish settlers were required to provide bawns and in some cases strong houses or castles, and Scottish architectural influences are strong. Typical are the round corbelled turrets with conical roofs, such as occur at Ballygally Castle in County Antrim. Most of the Plantation castles were destroyed in the 1641 rebellion, and thereafter there was little attempt to build fortified residences. Similarly the development of heavy artillery meant the end of building traditional castles. Ormond Castle at Carrick-on-Suir, County Tipperary, is one of the earliest examples of an Elizabethan mansion not built for defence. The best preserved Elizabethan town house is Rothe House in Kilkenny, built in 1594.

The star-shaped fort was developed in the seventeenth century to meet the challenge of artillery. Heavy earthworks form a strong outer perimeter, which is further guarded by the pointed bastions which give the fort its shape. A good example is at Charlemont, County Armagh. The first fortifications were erected during Mountjoy's campaign of 1602, the star fort being completed in 1624, and outer earthworks added in 1673. Another example is Charles Fort near Kinsale, County Cork.

Charles I's accession in 1625 was an opportunity to negotiate concessions for Catholics in return for a contribution to royal revenue. In return for a payment of £120,000 spread over three years a group of Old English peers was offered 'Graces', of which the most significant concerned land tenure and religion. The king guaranteed that no family would be dispossessed where it had occupied the land for more than sixty years. A simple oath of allegiance replaced the oath of supremacy for Catholics seeking to practise law, and wards of court could come into their inheritance without having to take the oath of supremacy. Although the king did not entirely fulfil his side of the bargain, for no parliament was called to make the Graces law, the Catholics enjoyed improved conditions for some years.

In 1633 Charles I made Sir Thomas Wentworth lord deputy. Wentworth set out to improve the royal revenue, and to increase royal power so that Ireland would be on the king's side in any future conflict with the English parliament. However, in playing one section of the populace off against another he ultimately succeeded in antagonising almost every element. Catholics distrusted him because he would not allow all the Graces to become law. He refused to confirm land titles more than sixty years old, and pressed a royal claim to Connacht with the intention of establishing a new plantation. He penalised undertakers in Ulster for not adhering strictly to the Articles of Plantation, and in Londonderry the London guilds were fined £70,000 as well as forfeiting their charter. In 1634 a convocation of the Church of Ireland accepted the Thirty-nine Articles of the Church of England, and Puritanism came under attack. The principal sufferers were Scottish Presbyterians in Ulster, and some ministers lost their livings and fled to Scotland. Presbyterians in Scotland rebelled in 1638, and the following year Wentworth tried to impose on Protestant Scots living in Ulster a 'black oath' submitting to the king's authority. Opposition to Wentworth's administration grew, and this helped the English parliament to have him attainted and executed. As the clash between king and parliament in England moved inevitably towards civil war, the native Irish saw an opportunity to regain their lost territory and independence.

The 1641 Rebellion

The plot to overthrow the government in Dublin was worked out by Rory O'More, whose family had lost land through the plantation of Laois, and a number of discontented northerners led by Sir Phelim O'Neill. They looked to the continent for assistance from Owen Roe O'Neill, a nephew of Hugh O'Neill who had served in the Spanish army, and from Father Luke Wadding, an eminent Franciscan in Rome. The first objective was to seize Dublin Castle and members of the government on 23 October 1641, but a drunkard disclosed the plan on the eve of its execution, and the proposed attack was thwarted. In Ulster, however, there were a number of simultaneous risings, and many planters were killed or forced to flee. The Irish captured a number of strongholds, and in others the besieged planters were soon short of food and water. O'Neill claimed that he was acting on the orders of Charles I and defending the king against parliament, and although this was untrue, it gravely damaged the king's cause in England and Scotland.

Within a few weeks, the Old English allied themselves with the native Irish and demanded freedom of religion. Within a year much of Ireland was in the hands of the rebels. By this time civil war had broken out in England. Charles raised his standard at Nottingham in August 1642, and in the same month a wholly Protestant parliament met in Dublin. Some Protestants remained loyal to the king, but others supported the

parliamentary cause in England. In Ulster a Scottish army under General Robert Monro had come to the aid of the planters, and acted under joint orders from the English and Scottish parliaments. In England an Act of parliament encouraged so-called 'Adventurers' to contribute money towards suppressing the rebellion, in return for which they would receive confiscated land.

In May 1642 leading Catholics met at Kilkenny and set up a provisional government. Plans were laid for a general assembly, which met in October, and this 'Confederation of Kilkenny' adopted the motto *Pro Deo, pro Rege, pro Patria Hibernia unanimis*. Unity proved elusive, however, for there were underlying differences between the Old English and the native Irish. Individual rivalries led to a division of the military command, with Owen Roe O'Neill leading the confederate army in Ulster and Thomas Preston, brother of Lord Gormanston, taking charge in Leinster.

Efforts to negotiate an effective truce proved abortive, and a confused war dragged on for several years. Although the Old English would have been satisfied to reach a moderate settlement with the king's representative, the Earl of Ormond, the native Irish were encouraged by a papal nuncio, Cardinal Rinuccini, to hope for an outright victory and a return of their lands. In 1646 Owen Roe O'Neill won a substantial victory over Monro at Benburb, but failed to press home his advantage in Ulster, and instead marched south to help install Rinuccini as president of the supreme council at Kilkenny. In July 1647 Ormond handed Dublin over to the forces of the English parliament and left the country. He returned a year later to attempt to unite the royalists in Ireland, and the execution of Charles I in 1649 actually stiffened Irish resistance to the English parliament. However, Ormond was defeated as he advanced on Dublin in August 1649, and two weeks later Oliver Cromwell arrived in the city.

Oliver Cromwell

The rebellion of 1641 had produced many stories of the barbarous massacre of Protestants, and the cruelty shown during Cromwell's nine months in Ireland was a form of revenge. He was also intent on a final defeat of the royalist cause in Ireland, and on exploiting the island to reward his victorious army. The Puritan leader had proved his military

Left: Dublin Castle

genius in the civil war, and the only comparable Irish commander, Owen Roe O'Neill, was a sick man who died before the year's end.

The 'Lord Lieutenant and General for the Parliament of England' began by storming Drogheda on 11 September 1649. The garrison refused to surrender, and Cromwell ordered that they be put to death as a warning to other towns. He then turned south and treated the garrison at Wexford in similar fashion. The last major resistance was at Clonmel, where Hugh O'Neill, a nephew of Owen Roe, fought bravely before escaping to Limerick with his army. Many more garrisons in Leinster and Munster submitted voluntarily, and the Catholic confederation gradually disintegrated. Cromwell sailed from Ireland on 26 May 1650, leaving his son-in-law, Henry Ireton, as lord lieutenant and commander. In October 1651 Limerick yielded to Ireton after a long siege, and in May 1652 Galway became the last major royalist stronghold to fall.

In August 1652 the 'Long Parliament' in England passed an Act of Settlement providing for large-scale forfeiture of land by any who had not shown 'their constant good affection to the Commonwealth of England' during the Irish rebellion. The leaders of the rebellion forfeited all land and property rights. A second group were allowed to retain a proportion of their landholding, but it had to be new land allocated to them in Connacht or Clare. Ten counties in the rest of Ireland were set aside, with the intention of allocating half the forfeited land to adventurers and half to soldiers. In the remaining counties the government could make use of forfeited land for a variety of useful purposes, and in practice much of this also went to soldiers.

Although all 'transplantable persons' were supposed to move west of the river Shannon by 1 May 1654 on pain of death, there were some delays before Cromwell's scheme was finally enforced. The plantation was not wholly successful, for the adventurers found (as earlier undertakers had) that they needed to retain Irish tenants. Many soldiers sold their land and returned to England, while those who remained often intermarried with the Irish and allowed their children to become Catholics. Moreover the plantation left a legacy of bitterness towards the English, and largely removed the traditional divisions and distinctions between the native Irish and the Old English. Catholic priests were outlawed, and those who remained in Ireland risked hanging or transportation to the West Indies, where many impoverished Irish had already been sold into slavery. The Church of Ireland also suffered, because of the Puritans' hatred of bishops, although less severely. Even the northern

Presbyterians were threatened for a time because they shared Scottish sympathy for the Stuart cause. Cromwell also abolished the Irish parliament, and Ireland instead sent thirty members to Westminster.

The Restoration

Cromwell died in September 1658, and in May 1660 Charles II was restored to the thrones of England, Scotland and Ireland. With the return of the monarchy the dispossessed Irish hoped for the return of their confiscated lands, but the Cromwellians were in a strong position in Ireland, and in any case the king's father, Charles I, had given royal assent to the Adventurers Act of 1642. An Irish parliament met in May 1661 and was dominated by Cromwellians. A year later it passed an Act of Settlement, which provided that those who could show their innocence should be restored to their estates, while any planters disturbed as a consequence would receive land elsewhere. The scheme proved difficult to execute, and was amended in 1665 by an Act of Explanation, which required adventurers and soldiers to give up one-third of their land. The Cromwellians accepted both acts reluctantly, but under Poynings' Law the Irish parliament had no power to alter legislation drawn up by the English council, and the settlers were confirmed in a substantial part of their holdings. Whereas Catholics held about three-fifths of Ireland in 1641, they had little over one-fifth after the Act of Explanation was implemented. They were again allowed to live in cities, but could not be members of the corporation, and they were in practice denied seats in parliament.

The Catholic Church began to re-organise, but throughout Charles's reign there were recurrences of anti-papist feeling. Oliver Plunkett, the Archbishop of Armagh, was executed in England in 1681 following the Popish Plot invented by Titus Oates. The Church of Ireland regained its estates under the Act of Settlement, and two new archbishops and ten bishops were consecrated in Dublin in January 1661. However, while it was recognised by parliament as the established church, its efforts to impose uniformity of religion met with little success. In the north some Presbyterian ministers were expelled from their livings by the Bishop of Down and Connor, Jeremy Taylor, but they were able to maintain the basic organisation of their church, and in 1672 received from Charles an annual *regium donum* or king's gift.

For much of Charles's reign the lord lieutenancy was held by the first Duke of Ormond, as the twelfth Earl had become. He was a Butler, one

of the Old English, but had been raised as a Protestant under crown wardship. When Charles died and was succeeded by his brother James II, a Catholic, Ormond was immediately deposed and the king appointed as lord lieutenant his brother-in-law, Lord Clarendon. A leading Irish Catholic, Colonel Richard Talbot, became lieutenant-general of the army with the title of Earl of Tyrconnell. He reorganised the army, replacing Protestants with Catholics, and gradually began to dominate Clarendon, who was a member of the Church of England. Catholics began to hold judgeships, sit on the privy council and gain places in town councils, and there was great Protestant apprehension when Tyrconnell was appointed lord lieutenant in 1687. Many soldiers and merchants left the country, and they helped to turn English opinion against the king and to persuade the Protestant William of Orange to accept the throne of England.

William of Orange

James II fled to France soon after William of Orange had landed in England. In February 1689 William III and his wife Mary II, daughter of James, accepted the crown of England as joint sovereigns with the approval of parliament. Soon afterwards James's Scottish supporters were defeated in battle, and Catholic Ireland remained his only hope. Tyrconnell hoped to hold Ireland for him, but in Ulster the towns of Londonderry and Enniskillen refused to admit royal troops. In March 1689 James arrived from France and marched with an army to Londonderry. The governor, Robert Lundy, was prepared to negotiate a surrender but the citizens insisted on resistance. A fifteen-week siege lasted until the end of July, when a relief ship broke through a Jacobite boom across the river Foyle to reach the starving town. Two weeks later Marshal Schomberg landed on the shores of Belfast Lough and captured Carrickfergus for William. The Protestant king himself arrived at Carrickfergus in June 1690, and immediately marched south.

James had summoned a largely Catholic parliament in Dublin in 1689, and this 'patriot parliament' passed a number of measures to restore Catholic power. By the time James had marched to meet William's army, he had forfeited any hope of Protestant support, and Ireland's future was bound to be decided on the battlefield. The armies met at the river Boyne on 1 July 1690 (12 July in modern calendars), and

Left: William of Orange, Carrickfergus

William's larger force triumphed over James's French and Irish troops. James fled to France, leaving his commanders to retreat to the river Shannon, where Athlone and Limerick became their main strongholds. Patrick Sarsfield, the leading Jacobite general, held Limerick against William's onslaught, and the king finally withdrew and returned to England. The Dutch General Ginkel took charge of the Williamite forces, and in 1691 he captured Athlone and won a decisive battle at nearby Aughrim. Limerick withstood a second siege for a month before Sarsfield negotiated a treaty, under which the Irish soldiers had the choice of taking an oath of allegiance to William and returning to their homes, joining the English army or sailing to France. Most of them chose exile, and during the following century many 'wild geese' left Ireland to joint the Irish brigades of Europe's armies. Ginkel became Earl of Athlone, and was one of the beneficiaries of the Williamite plantation, which left about one-seventh of Ireland in Catholic hands.

The Protestant Nation

The Ascendancy

The success of the Williamite cause left Ireland in the hands of a Protestant ascendancy, that is to say the 'English in Ireland' who were largely the descendants of the Tudor and Stuart settlers. The Old English and the native Irish had little or no hope of regaining land or influence, and for more than a century they suffered grievously from penal measures designed to buttress the colonists' grip on Ireland. An English Act of 1691 was extended to Ireland, requiring members of the Irish parliament to subscribe to a declaration against Roman Catholic doctrines. When the Treaty of Limerick was eventually confirmed by parliament in 1697, it was in a much altered form. Parliament also passed acts for the disarming of 'papists' and the banishment of Catholic bishops.

William III was in no position to impose tolerant policies on the Irish parliament, for he depended on the Protestant ascendancy to keep Ireland at peace. Consequently parliament became increasingly influential, with its control of taxation the most powerful weapon it could use against a needy government. The government was headed by the lord lieutenant or, in his absence, two or three lords justice. Parliament was still restricted by the provisions of Poynings' Law, and it could not meet or pass any law without the full approval of the king and his council in England. In 1720 a further Act known as the Sixth of George I gave the English parliament the right to pass legislation binding on Ireland without the agreement of the Irish parliament. However, the practice grew in the 1690s of drawing up 'heads of bills' or legislative proposals, and these were sent to the privy council in England in the hope that they would be put to the Westminster parliament. This gave the Irish parliament a new initiative in devising legislation. In addition by limiting the duration of tax provisions to two years at a time, parliament ensured that it would be summoned much more often than in the past.

The Penal Laws

Laws penalising religious beliefs had been common in Western Europe since the Reformation. Ireland's penal laws were unusual in that they were directed, not against a religious minority like the Huguenots in

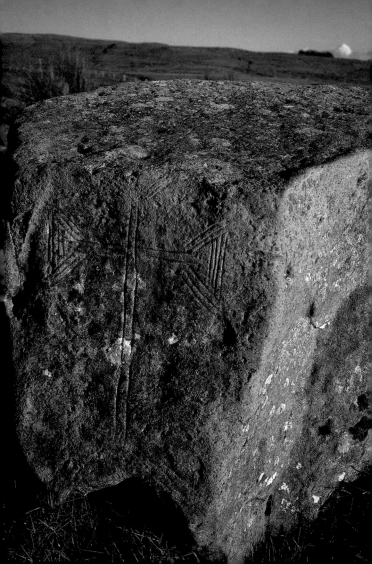

France, but against the majority of the population. In addition the object was not so much to convert Catholics as to reduce them to impotent subservience. In time, and particularly by the Hanoverian Georges, the laws which interfered with religious worship tended to fall into disuse. By contrast there was rigorous enforcement of those provisions which prevented Catholics bettering themselves socially or economically.

Roman Catholics were excluded from parliament, from the armed forces, from any kind of government service, and from entering the legal profession. They could not teach or maintain schools, and it was illegal to send children abroad to be educated. They could not hold arms to protect themselves from 'rapparees' (outlaw bands) or highwaymen, and could not own a horse worth more than £5. No Catholic was allowed to buy land, and leases were restricted to thirty-one years.

There was pressure on the wealthier Catholics to join the Church of Ireland, and many landowners and professional men did change their religion. In the case of landowners the eldest son could inherit the whole estate only if he became a Protestant. Otherwise the land was divided equally among the male heirs, with the result that Catholic landholdings steadily diminished in size. Where wealthy Catholics adhered to their religion and tried to evade the law, there was the risk of being exposed by 'discoverers' who were rewarded for proving breaches of the law. However, many chose to send their sons to Irish colleges on the continent, and often these children did not return to an island which offered so few outlets for their talents. In time poor Catholics tended to look to their clergy for political leadership rather than to the depleted ranks of Catholic merchants and landowners.

In 1697 the Irish parliament passed an Act banishing Catholic bishops and regular or monastic clergy, and a further of this nature was passed in 1703. Provision was made for parish priests to be registered, subject to an oath of allegiance, and more than one thousand took this opportunity to carry out their work within the law. However, there was no provision for priests entering Ireland from abroad, and in the absence of bishops to ordain Irish clergy the number of priests was theoretically bound to decline. In practice, however, some bishops remained in Ireland, often in disguise, and eventually others joined them. The regular clergy gradually returned to Ireland, and monasteries were restored. There was always a fear that religious persecution might follow some new wave of

Left: Mass rock at Dunteige in the Glens of Antrim

anti-papist feeling among the Ascendancy, but the Church quietly continued its work in modest chapels or even in the open air at 'Mass rocks'.

The Dissenters

The northern Presbyterians were also victims of religious discrimination despite their support for the Williamite cause. Dissenters had fewer grievances than their Catholic neighbours because their property rights were not curtailed and they could carry arms and vote in elections. However, their creed was not recognised by the state, and marriages performed by Presbyterian clergy could be ruled illegal and the children of such marriages illegitimate. In 1704, an Act against Popery required office-holders under the crown to take the sacrament according to the Church of Ireland, and this excluded Presbyterians from civil service and military posts which had been open to them since 1691. At the same time they lost control of municipal corporations in the North. The *regium donum* was suspended towards the end of Queen Anne's reign, but restored under George I in 1718. The following year a Toleration Act freed Presbyterians from the obligation to attend the Established Church, and they were allowed to worship freely, although still required to pay tithes to the Church of England. During the eighteenth century many Presbyterians emigrated to North America in search of religious freedom, and their resistance to English rule was an important factor in the War of Independence.

The Irish Economy

The century of peace which followed the Williamite victory might have been expected to encourage economic growth and prosperity. However, most of the population lived in poverty, and not until the last quarter of the eighteenth century was there substantial improvement. The policy of the Westminster parliament was to restrict Irish trade where it might offer competition to English manufacturers and merchants. Thus in 1699 the export of Irish woollens was prohibited except to England, where there were heavy duties to pay. Irish manufacturers had begun to find markets on the continent, but they were now in practice confined to the Irish market and some smuggling. The linen industry grew in importance, largely because skilled French Huguenot refugees had settled in Ulster, and there were no important English manufacturers to demand curbs.

The Irish brewing industry began to expand, but contracted after legislation compelling the importation of hops from Great Britain alone. Another industry declined when in 1746 the export of Irish glass was prohibited. The provisions trade flourished after the export of live cattle was forbidden, and salted beef, butter, hide and tallow were shipped to Europe and to the West Indies. However, the export of provisions and the smuggling of wool both encouraged an increase in pasture at the expense of arable land which might have fed a growing population.

Irish agriculture was woefully inefficient by comparison with that of England, and the principal cause was the system of land tenure. Many of the landlords were absentees, preferring to live in England while their Irish estates were leased to 'squireens' who divided the land among tenant farmers. Often these farms were sub-divided, so that holdings were small and rents were pushed up so that all the middlemen could make a handsome profit. Few landlords attempted to improve their land or the standard of agriculture, and tenants had little incentive, except in Ulster where by custom the tenant enjoyed greater security of tenure and could actually sell his interest or 'tenant right'.

Jonathan Swift, Dean of Saint Patrick's Cathedral in Dublin from 1713 to 1745, was an outspoken critic of English rule. In 1720 he wrote anonymously *A Proposal for the Universal Use of Irish Manufactures*, and the government tried unsuccessfully to prosecute the printer for publishing a seditious pamphlet. In 1724, while engaged on *Gulliver's Travels*, he published the first of a series of *Drapier's Letters* in which he assumed the guise of a Dublin businessman and criticised a proposal to give an Englishman named William Wood the right to mint copper coins for Ireland at a substantial profit. 'Wood's halfpence' were abandoned in the ensuing controversy, and Swift went on to challenge England's right to legislate for Ireland. In *The Querist*, first published in 1735, the Protestant Bishop of Cloyne, George Berkeley, also posed pointed questions about Ireland's economy.

The eighteenth century also saw the emergence of secret societies in rural Ireland. When restrictions on the importation of Irish cattle and beef in England were lifted in 1758-9, landlords were encouraged to extend their pastures and to fence commons on which peasants had traditionally grazed their animals. In Munster the Whiteboys (disguised in white smocks) destroyed fences and livestock at night, and protected peasants against extortionate tithes. Other local grievances produced

Above: The Gothic front of Castle Ward

societies such as the Hearts of Oak and Hearts of Steel in Ulster, and the Molly Maguires. Although their methods were often violent and they did not always have the support of local peasants, the societies flourished in spite of repressive government measures.

The Patriot Party

As the eighteenth century progressed, there emerged in the Irish parliament an opposition group, commonly called 'patriots', who were united principally in seeking greater independence from England. Their numbers fluctuated, but they were always capable of embarrassing the government, and in 1753 parliament rejected a Money Bill which acknowledged the king's right to dispose of a surplus of revenue. In 1768 an Octennial Act provided for a general election at least every eight years. Hitherto a parliament had lasted throughout a king's reign, so there was now more chance of public opinion influencing members. The leadership of the patriots had passed to Henry Flood, a powerful orator who entered parliament in 1759, but in 1775 he wearied of opposition and took government office in the hope that 'a patriot may do as much in office as out of it'. His successor was a young lawyer, Henry Grattan, who was quickly able to capitalise on events outside Ireland.

The Big House

William of Orange's victories in Ireland preceded a century of peace, and from about 1720 onwards this was reflected in the ambitious building ventures of prosperous landlords. Labour was cheap, and the owners of vast demesnes could afford to import building materials and employ the finest architects to create the 'big houses' that symbolised the Protestant ascendancy. One of the earliest was Castletown House near Celbridge, County Kildare. Built around 1722 for the Speaker of the Irish Commons, William Conolly, it consists of a three-storey central block linked by curving colonnades to side wings. The Palladian exterior and the rococo interior are typical of the eighteenth century, and the house now forms the headquarters of the Irish Georgian Society. Russborough House, near Blessington, County Wicklow, is another fine example of Palladian architecture. Its designer, Richard Cassels, was also responsible for Westport House in County Mayo, which is open to the public. Among the houses built later in the century, Castle Coole near Enniskillen, County Fermanagh, is owned by the National Trust. The classical Georgian façades eventually gave way to Gothic-revival styles. Castle Ward House, near Strangford, County Down, was built about 1765 and has one Palladian front and one Gothic front.

The American War of Independence, which began in April 1775, was closely watched by the patriots, who sought the same sort of financial and economic independence as the American colonists. Much of the army was withdrawn to fight in America, and when France and Spain joined with the colonists in 1778, an invasion of Ireland was feared. The patriots proposed the formation of an armed militia, and with government approval there were soon companies of Volunteers throughout the island. The Volunteers were Protestants, and they quickly turned their attention to political issues. They made a point of having uniforms of Irish cloth, and non-importation associations were formed to encourage the purchase of Irish goods. On 4 November 1779 the Volunteers celebrated William III's birthday with a parade outside parliament and carried placards demanding free trade. The following month Lord North, the British prime minister, removed most of the curbs on Irish trade.

There followed on 15 February 1782 a convention of Volunteers at Dungannon, County Tyrone, which gave further voice to the demands of the emergent Protestant nation. Grattan's oratory swept the Irish parliament into a new demand for independence, granted by the Whig government which, under Lord Rockingham, had replaced North's Tories. The Westminster parliament repealed the Sixth of George I, and the Irish parliament substantially modified Poynings' Law, leaving only a royal right to veto but not alter legislation.

Grattan's Parliament

Ireland's parliamentary independence lasted only until the Acts of Union in 1800. It was a period of commercial prosperity, and with important new buildings springing up Dublin felt itself more than ever a capital city. However, while it is customary to refer to 'Grattan's parliament', the patriot leader was unable to maintain his hold on the majority of members who represented 'pocket boroughs' (where a wealthy patron nominated the member) and 'rotten boroughs' (where there were few or no inhabitants). In addition the administration remained in the hands of a lord lieutenant responsible to the government in England.

Within the patriots Grattan's leadership was quickly challenged by the jealous Henry Flood, who questioned whether Westminster had sufficiently ceded its authority. Flood ultimately forced a Renunciation Act which in 1783 affirmed Ireland's legislative and judicial independence. In November 1783 Flood dominated a convention of Volunteers in Dublin, and a scheme was drawn up for the reform of parliament. It would have got rid of rotten boroughs, prevented corporations returning members and given Protestant leaseholders the vote, but parliament rejected the scheme and the Volunteers ceased to have political influence. The unity of the Protestant nation had been seriously impaired, however, and there was a dangerous disrespect for parliamentary institutions. In addition, while parliament in 1782 passed legislation freeing Catholics from restrictions in such matters as education and land purchase, no move was made to extend Catholics' political rights.

Above: Grattan's Parliament

Henry Grattan

Born 1746, son of a wealthy lawyer and landowner who became Recorder of Dublin and a member of the Irish parliament. Grattan himself became a lawyer, but showed more interest in writing political articles. He was nominated to a pocket borough in 1775, and his oratory quickly established him as leader of the patriot party. By 1782 he had successfully campaigned for the removal of trade restrictions and for the independence of the Irish parliament under the Crown. Although a member of the Protestant ascendancy, Grattan saw himself as the leader of a united nation, and argued that 'the Irish Protestant should never be free until the Irish Catholic ceased to be a slave'. The Penal Laws were eased, but parliament was unwilling to give Catholics equal rights. Corruption flourished, and the administration in Dublin Castle continued much as before. A sick and disappointed man, Grattan saw his hopes finally dashed by the parliamentary union with Great Britain. He rose from a sickbed to oppose the Bill of Union in 1800, and spoke for two hours sitting down. In 1805 he was elected to Westminster, where he pleaded the cause of Catholic emancipation until his death in 1820.

Above: This monument in Castlebar is made up of pikes, the weapon of choice for the Irish revolutionaries in 1792. Castlebar itself was the site of battle during the revolution.

Anglo-Irish relations were also in a turbulent state. William Pitt the Younger became Tory prime minister in 1783, and a year later proposed a trade agreement between Britain and Ireland. His proposals would have given Ireland almost equal trading rights, but Pitt was forced to make concessions to English merchants and the amended version was dropped in face of Irish opposition. In 1788 George III became insane, and Westminster debated the appointment of a regent. At the same time the Irish parliament claimed the right to appoint a regent for Ireland, so that there was a possibility that the two islands might have different rulers. A crisis was averted by the king's recovery, but Pitt began to consider seriously the case for a full union of Britain and Ireland.

The United Irishmen

The French Revolution, which broke out in 1789, was watched closely in Ireland, and republican ideas began to spread. The fall of the Bastille was celebrated in Belfast, and northern Presbyterians pressed for parliamentary reform and religious equality for all. A young Protestant lawyer in Dublin, Theobald Wolfe Tone, published a pamphlet called *An Argument on behalf of the Catholics of Ireland*, and was invited to Belfast. There on 14 October 1791 he and some influential northerners founded the Society of United Irishmen. A branch was formed in Dublin before the year ended. The United Irishmen began as debating societies, publishing a series of demands for reform, and a conciliatory Pitt pressed the Irish government into accepting Relief Acts which in 1792 and 1793 gave Catholics the vote but not the right to sit in parliament or as judges.

Theobald Wolfe Tone

Born in Dublin in 1763, son of a coachmaker who inherited property in Bodenstown, County Kildare. He was at Trinity College, Dublin, when the nearby Irish parliament achieved its independence in 1782. After an elopement Tone completed his legal studies in 1789. He hoped for a political career, and began writing pamphlets, including An Argument on behalf of the Catholics of Ireland in 1791. Presbyterian radicals invited Tone to Belfast, and the Society of United Irishmen was founded there. Although a Protestant, Tone was appointed assistant secretary of the Central Catholic Committee, a reform body, in 1792.

In 1794 the United Irishmen were suppressed and became an underground revolutionary movement. Tone managed to avoid the charge of treason, but was forced to exile himself to America. In 1796 he sailed for France, and persuaded the revolutionary leaders to invade Ireland. Tone was commissioned in the French army, but bad weather foiled the expedition. Rebellion broke out in Ireland in 1798, but failed. Tone was captured when a French fleet surrendered in Lough Swilly, and was tried for treason. He cut his own throat when his request to be shot like a soldier was refused. His death is commemorated each year at Bodenstown, where he is buried, and he is remembered as the first true republican, a man who sought 'to substitute the common name of Irishman in place of the denominations of Protestant, Catholic and Dissenter'.

Above: Entrance to St Stephen's Green

England and France were soon at war, and Tone looked to France for help in asserting Ireland's independence. Attempts were made to suppress the United Irishmen, who quickly formed a secret organisation bound by oaths and intent on revolution. At the same time the Protestant Orange Society (later Orange Order) emerged in Ulster with the objective of maintaining the Protestant ascendancy. There had been a decade of strife because of competition for land, and in 1795 the Protestant Peep o' Day Boys defeated Catholic Defenders in a pitched battle at the Diamond, a village in County Armagh. The Orange Society which they founded was blamed for subsequent persecution of Catholics, and the United Irishmen won many recruits from the Catholic peasantry and from Protestants who were horrified by the religious strife.

Dublin and Other Cities

The eighteenth century was Dublin's golden age, and many noble buildings were erected. The population grew rapidly, and the city spread into graceful squares bounded by stately terraces whose interiors were handsomely adorned by stucco workers, woodcarvers, and other craftsmen. Parliament House was completed in 1739, enlarged later in the century, and after the Union became the Bank of Ireland. Nearby Leinster House was designed by Cassels for the Earl of Kildare. It was begun in 1745, looks more a country house than a town house, and was later occupied for more than a century by the Royal Dublin Society before it was purchased for the modern Irish parliament. Behind Leinster House is Merrion Square, most beautiful of Dublin Squares and second in size only to St Stephen's Green. Trinity College was largely reconstructed in the eighteenth century and little of the earlier buildings remain. The parliamentary independence of the last two decades of the century was accompanied by further architectural masterpieces in Dublin. The outstanding architect was James Gandon, whose work includes the Custom House, the Four Courts and the Kings Inns.

Elsewhere in Ireland, cities proclaimed their prosperity with elegant Georgian buildings and wide paved streets. Cork, Limerick and Waterford retain much of the grandeur they acquired during the eighteenth century.

In February 1796 an Insurrection Act gave magistrates powers to search for arms and to hang anyone administering an illegal oath, and later in the year the government supplemented the army's strength with a Protestant yeomanry. In December Tone accompanied a French fleet to Bantry Bay, but high winds prevented troops landing. In March 1797 an army under General Lake was sent to disarm Ulster, and his soldiers committed many atrocities. The mission was highly successful, however, and with the betrayal of a number of Leinster leaders only a small band of dedicated revolutionaries remained to launch the rebellion in May 1798. In Ulster only Antrim and Down rose against the government, and the rebels were soon defeated. There was more success in County Wexford, where the leaders were Catholic clergy, but the slaughter of many Protestants suggested a religious war rather than true adherence to the ideals of Tone. The rebellion was virtually over by the time French expeditions arrived at Killala Bay, County Mayo, in August and at Lough Swilly in September. Both were defeated and Tone himself was captured in the second and condemned for high treason. He was sentenced to be hanged, drawn and quartered, and when his request to be shot was refused, he committed suicide. Although the '98 Rising had failed, Tone left behind a tradition of violence which has marked the subsequent course of Irish republicanism.

The Acts of Union

Pitt was now convinced that a union of Ireland and Great Britain was essential if further rebellion was to be avoided and the Protestant ascendancy maintained. When the Irish parliament met in January 1799, it rejected a government proposal to consider a scheme of union, but the majority was narrow and the chief secretary, Lord Castlereagh, set about reversing the decision by methods which included bribery and intimidation. Those in government office had to support the union or resign, while others were given jobs or titles in return for support. Many seats changed hands, as the government bought out opponents of union. When parliament assembled in January 1800, the government was assured of success, despite a moving plea from the ailing Grattan, dressed in Volunteer uniform. On 1 August royal assent was given to a measure bringing to an end five centuries of parliamentary activity. An identical Act of Union was passed by Westminster, and the two measures came into force on 1 January 1801.

Under this legislation Ireland was joined with Great Britain in the United Kingdom of Great Britain and Ireland. At Westminster, Ireland was to be represented in the Lords by twenty-eight peers (elected for life by the Irish peers) and four bishops of the Established Church, and in the Commons by 100 members out of a total of 660. The Church of England and the Church of Ireland were united as a single Established Church. There was to be free trade between the two islands, except for some manufactured goods such as woollen and cotton cloth on which customs duties could remain for twenty years. The financial systems of the two islands were to remain separate, except that Ireland was to contribute two-seventeenths of expenditure on defence and other joint services. Existing laws remained in effect in the respective islands, but could be altered by the Westminster parliament.

Ireland under the Union

Catholic Emancipation

The spirit of the United Irishmen was not wholly dead, and the younger brother of an exiled leader of the '98 Rising planned a new insurrection. Robert Emmet hoped to seize Dublin Castle, but his organisation was faulty and the rebellion in 1803 ended as little more than a street brawl. Emmet was captured, however, and his speech from the dock at his trial became an inspiration to later generations seeking Irish freedom. 'When my country takes her place among the nations of the earth,' he ended, 'then, and not till then, let my epitaph be written.'

For some years political life declined and the government's major concern was the agrarian disorders fomented by secret societies like the Ribbonmen, the Whiteboys and the Threshers. The government at Westminster passed Coercion Acts giving strong powers to deal with wrongdoers or suspects, and the life of the Irish peasant became increasingly cheerless, particularly as the end of the Napoleonic wars in 1815 led to an economic slump. The population of rural Ireland was rising, holdings were being subdivided, and periodic failures of the potato crop brought about very great distress.

It was the issue of Catholic emancipation which first gave Ireland's Catholics a sense of unity and potential power. Pitt had led the Catholic hierarchy to believe that the Act of Union would be followed by legislation giving Irish Catholics the right to sit at Westminster, but neither the bishops nor the remaining Catholic aristocracy protested when nothing was done. It was left to a Catholic barrister, Daniel O'Connell, to form in 1823 a Catholic Association which aimed not only at full political rights but also at furthering Catholic interests generally. O'Connell was a commanding orator, capable of organising and dominating large open-air meetings, and the association was widely supported through a penny-a-month subscription scheme.

The Association's first victory was in the 1826 general election, when it successfully backed a Protestant candidate in County Waterford against Lord George Beresford, whose family owned much of the county. In 1828 O'Connell himself was successful in a by-election in County Clare. He was unable to take his seat because of the Oath of Supremacy, but opinion in Westminster had been veering towards emancipation and within a year a Catholic Relief Bill received the royal assent. However, while the Oath of

Supremacy was replaced by one acceptable to Catholics and all but the highest public offices were open to them, additional measures were designed to limit the Catholic victory. The Catholic Association was suppressed, and the qualification for voting was raised from £2 to £10 freehold, so that the forty-shilling freeholders who had backed O'Connell were disfranchised.

Robert Emmet

Born 1778, son of a prosperous doctor who worked among Dublin's poor, and younger brother of a leading United Irishman, Thomas Addis Emmet. Expelled from Trinity College, Dublin, in 1798, he later joined his brother in France, where he hoped to interest Napoleon Bonaparte in assisting a new insurrection. He returned to Dublin in 1802, and spent his own fortune on providing weapons, including a rocket. He was assisted by two notable Ulstermen, Thomas Russell and Jemmy Hope, but greatly overestimated the popular support a rising could command. An attempt to seize Dublin Castle in 1803 failed, and after escaping to the Wicklow Mountains Emmet was betrayed and hanged. His speech from the dock is a classic call for freedom.

Daniel O'Connell

Born 1775, son of a small landlord in County Kerry. As a Catholic he was not allowed to attend Trinity College, Dublin, so he was educated in France and England before becoming one of the first Catholic barristers in Ireland. He took no part in the 1798 rising, but spoke against the Act of Union and began to agitate for Catholic emancipation. In 1823 he founded the Catholic Association, and quickly became a national figure. In 1828 he won a by-election in County Clare. A year later the British government conceded Catholics the right to sit in parliament. A flamboyant figure known as 'The Liberator', O'Connell entertained freely and was often in debt. In 1840 he formed the National Repeal Association to restore the Irish parliament, but this time constitutional methods failed and he lost influence after he accepted a government ban on a proposed rally at Clontarf in 1843. He was imprisoned for three months in 1844 on a conspiracy charge, which was ultimately quashed, and his health suffered. He died in Italy in 1847.

Left: Daniel O'Connell Statue, Dublin

Reform and Repeal

During the eighteenth century Irish nationalism had been a Protestant movement. Daniel O'Connell, who became known as 'The Liberator', had shown that a mass movement of Catholics, involving peasants and priests, could bring effective pressure on the government in a peaceful and orderly way. Although he sought repeal of the Acts of Union, his first experience of Westminster led him to believe that there was more immediate hope of winning reforms in such matters as tithes, education and the relief of poverty. For most of the 1830s there was a Whig government in power, and in Britain's 'Age of Reform' the Whigs counted on support from O'Connell and his followers at Westminster.

Irish Reform was slow, however, and O'Connell was disappointed that the great Reform Act of 1832 did not restore the forty-shilling freehold vote. A tithe war broke out in Leinster in 1830, and spread to other provinces as large numbers of police and military were called in to enforce collection of taxes due to the Established Church. It was 1838 before a Tithe Act brought peace by converting tithe charges into rents and reducing them by one-quarter. A major reform was the establishment of a National Education Board in 1831, and within a decade there was an impressive system of 'national schools'. Hopes of educating Catholics and Protestants together were largely disappointed, however, and the use of the English language and English textbooks brought a steady decline in the Irish language. In 1838 the English Poor Law system was extended to Ireland, and the country was divided into Poor Law districts or unions, each with a workhouse managed by a board of guardians. It was a degrading system, which divided families and often forced peasants to give up their land and enter the workhouse when their real need was for temporary assistance. Nevertheless the administration at Dublin Castle enjoyed a new popularity among Catholics, largely because of a tolerant under-secretary, Thomas Drummond. A Scotsman, he held office from 1835 to 1840, and was largely responsible for organising a national police force, the Royal Irish Constabulary. He abandoned coercive measures, involved more Catholics in the administration of justice and did much to break the power of the Orange Order.

By 1840 it was clear to O'Connell that the Whig government under Lord Melbourne would soon give way to a less sympathetic Tory administration under Sir Robert Peel. Drummond died prematurely, and O'Connell decided to press the repeal issue. In April 1840 he formed the

National Repeal Association. After a slow start the movement was backed by Archbishop MacHale of Tuam and a number of bishops, and O'Connell held mass meetings as impressive as in the campaign for Catholic emancipation. His language became increasingly inflammatory and eventually the government called his bluff by banning a meeting due to be held on 8 October 1843 at Clontarf, the scene of Brian Boru's great victory. O'Connell, a man who believed in constitutional methods, immediately gave way. He was now in his late sixties, and he never recovered his former dominance.

Young Ireland

Some of the early support for O'Connell's Repeal Association had come from a group of journalists who became known as 'Young Ireland', and it was to them that Irish nationalism now turned for inspiration. Their weekly journal, the *Nation*, was first published in October 1842, and their concept of an Irish nationality which embraced everyone living in the island was at odds with O'Connell's nationalism, which tended to be Catholic in nature. The Young Ireland leaders were mostly Protestants, whose heroes were the men of 1798.

The most talented was Thomas Davis, a Dublin barrister, Protestant son of an English army surgeon (who died a month earlier) and an Anglo-Irish mother. He studied law at Trinity College, Dublin, and became a leading debater, along with a Catholic student, John Blake Dillon. In 1841 they both joined O'Connell's National Repeal Association, and in 1842 launched a newspaper, the *Nation*, with Catholic journalist Charles Gavan Duffy, who was to be editor. Davis's nationalism embraced all creeds and classes, and there emerged a group of 'Young Irelanders' who became disenchanted with O'Connell, who spoke so much of 'Old Ireland'.

Thomas Davis' poetry was very popular, and his teaching towards the end of a short life inspired the patriots of later generations. One of the unanswered questions of Irish history is whether he would have endorsed the use of force in the 1848 rising. Only thirty-one when he died of scarlet fever in 1845, he left his own epitaph: 'He served his country and loved his kind'.

The editor of the *Nation* was a Catholic journalist from County Monaghan, Charles Gavan Duffy, who believed that an Irish parliamentary party could be most effective by remaining independent of the Whigs and Tories alike. He published many fine poems and ballads,

Above: The Black Valley, Killarney was abandoned during the Famine

in some of which the Gaelic tradition was translated into English, while in others Tone and his colleagues were honoured. A famous ballad asked: 'Who fears to speak of Ninety-eight?'

The split with O'Connell developed after the 1843 failure, for the Young Irelanders were unable to accept his contention that physical force should never be used in the struggle for independence. John Mitchel, a solicitor from County Down, founded a new journal called the *United Irishman* and prepared for an armed rebellion. He was greatly influenced by the ideas of James Fintan Lalor, who argued that the cause of independence must be linked with the more practical attack on the evils of landlordism. The success of the French revolution of 1848 persuaded some of the Young Irelanders that an Irish uprising might succeed, but Mitchel was arrested on a charge of sedition, and one brief skirmish in County Tipperary put paid to the other rebels in August. Some escaped to America, while others were transported to Van Diemen's Land. Mitchel later escaped and went to America, where he published a famous *Jail Journal*. In retrospect it is clear that a rebellion had no chance of success in 1848, for thousands were dying of starvation in the great potato famine and had no will to fight. Yet the writings of the Young Ireland movement became a major influence on later generations.

The Great Famine

The population of Ireland had risen from about 5 million in 1800 to more than 8 million when potato blight reached Counties Wexford and Waterford from England in September 1845. There had been earlier famines, either brief in duration or localised in their impact, and people were used to such suffering. However, the great famine lasted until 1849, and no part of the island was unaffected. By 1851 the population had fallen by some 2 million, half of whom died while the other half emigrated.

The blight was a fungus growth rather than a disease of the potato itself, and it caused the potatoes to rot in the ground and give off an abominable smell. The Tory prime minister, Sir Robert Peel, appointed a commission to examine the disease, but it had no success. He also took swift relief measures, purchasing £100,000 worth of Indian corn and meal in America to prevent food prices from rising. Relief committees were organised and public works were begun so that people could earn money to buy food. The administration of Peel's measures was in the hands of the assistant secretary to the Treasury, Charles Trevelyan, who was unsympathetic to the principle of government aid. When a Whig government under Lord John Russell took office in 1846, *laissez-faire* ideas prevailed, and it was decided not to buy any more food. The potato crop failed again, and the winter of 1846-7 was one of the worst in living memory. Public works continued, but food itself was scarce. Through voluntary effort, in which Quakers played a major part, soup kitchens were established. Many died, however, either through starvation, or through exposure to bitter weather or through disease. Typhus and relapsing fever were both described as 'famine fever', and scurvy and dysentery were common. The government eventually recognised its errors, and public works were replaced by direct relief, in the hope that its cost would eventually be borne by the boards of guardians out of the Poor Law

rate. Those Irish who emigrated often died of disease at sea, sank in what were called 'coffin ships' or reached America too weak to survive.

The Nineteenth Century

The cataclysmic event of the nineteenth century was the great famine of the 1840s, and it has left its mark on the landscape in different ways. Emigration and death reduced the rural population substantially, and in western areas in particular one can see traces of fields once cultivated and derelict cottages. At this period there were still parts where the rundale or open-field system survived, and land held in common was re-allocated annually in small and inefficient plots. The famine opened the way to the consolidation of holdings, as had occurred elsewhere. The clachans or clusters of peasant houses began to disappear, and 'strip farms' became common, each stretching from the mountain pasture to the lowland bog. Fields now left to grass often reveal the shape of the 'lazy-beds' or ridges in which potatoes were grown. The relief works of the famine period included roads, harbours and even the substantial walls which commonly surround demesnes.

The nineteenth century also saw a growing contrast between Ulster and the other Irish provinces. Perhaps because there was already a domestic linen industry, Ulster seized the opportunities of the Industrial Revolution, and its new mills and shipyards brought with them terraces of cheap housing. Belfast is essentially a Victorian city, and few eighteenth-century buildings survive. The subsequent decline of the linen industry is marked by empty red-brick mills in many towns and villages of Ulster.

The long-term effects of the great famine were immense. The upward trend of population was reversed, and a countryside once full of young people was replaced by one in which emigration and late marriage were the rule. The traditional hostility between landlord and tenant was intensified, for many landlords had ignored the plight of their tenants and even engaged in large-scale eviction. There was resentment of the British government's inadequate measures, and Irish nationalists had a new bitterness towards their English neighbours.

Left: Statue of Annie Moore and her two brothers, the first Irish emigrants to pass through Ellis Island, New York before entering the United States

The Fenian Movement

The ideas of the Young Ireland movement had been preserved by the refugees who fled from Ireland after the 1848 rising failed. Two of them, James Stephens and John O'Mahony, settled in Paris, and in that revolutionary climate planned the overthrow of British rule by force. James Stephens was born in Kilkenny in 1824, son of a clerk. A civil engineer, he worked on the building of the Limerick and Waterford Railway, joining in the Young Ireland rising of 1848. He escaped with wounds from an affray at Ballingarry, County Tipperary.

Stephens returned to Ireland in 1856 and, after assurances of American backing from O'Mahony, who had since moved to New York, founded a secret society known variously as the Fenian Brotherhood, the Irish Republican Brotherhood (a title firmly established after a re-organisation of the republican movement in 1873) and 'the Organisation' on St Patrick's Day, 17 March 1858.

The name 'Fenian' derived from the legendary Finn MacCool's *fian* or band of warriors, and the society was wholly committed to force. Stephens quickly won recruits, notably from branches of the Phoenix Society, formed by O'Donovan Rossa in 1856 to discuss politics and literature. The Fenian Brotherhood was also launched in New York in 1858. Stephens sailed to America later in the year but was disappointed by his reception, the movement suffering thereafter from internal jealousies.

The Fenians believed in a revolution 'sooner or never', and counted on money from America to buy arms. Although the movement was intended to be secret, the self-indulgent Stephens returned to Ireland and launched a newspaper called the *Irish People* in 1863 to propagate his views. Fenianism was severely criticised by the Catholic Church and by other nationalist movements which it hoped to supplant. The American Civil War provided a valuable training ground for Irish soldiers and, when it ended in April 1865, Stephens laid plans for an insurrection later in the year. In September the government raided the office of the *Irish People* and arrested several Fenian leaders. Stephens resisted advice to launch the insurrection then and he was soon captured. He escaped from prison and fled to France. From there he went to America but his reluctance to begin the Rising led to his being deposed as head of the Fenian movement in 1867. Stephens returned to France and spent most of the rest of his life working as a journalist.

In the meantime, the government took the opportunity to arrest suspects, seize arms and send out of Ireland army units thought to have Fenian sympathisers. When the promised insurrection eventually took place on 5 March 1867, after some false starts, it was easily quelled. The rising had failed as Stephens had anticipated but he was unable to regain his former dictatorial hold on the movement. He eventually returned to Dublin in 1891 and died in 1901.

The Fenians were also active among the Irish in England, who had grown in number since the Famine. An attempt to capture Chester Castle and seize arms failed, and in September 1867 two leading Fenians were arrested. In a successful rescue attempt in Manchester a police constable was killed, and three suspects who pleaded their innocence were tried and hanged for the murder. The execution of the 'Manchester martyrs' heightened anti-English feeling in Ireland and among the Irish Americans. In the same way anti-Irish feelings were aroused in England by the killing of the constable and by an attempt in December 1867 to rescue a Fenian from Clerkenwell Prison in London, when an explosion killed more than twenty people. At the same time the incidents led some Englishmen to wonder whether there was room for greater reform and conciliation in the government's Irish policies. One of these was William Ewart Gladstone, soon to be prime minister.

Gladstone in Office

The 1861 census had shown that fewer than 700,000 people out of an Irish population of almost 6 million belonged to the Established Church in Ireland. In 1868 Gladstone pressed the case for disestablishing the Church, and gained power by winning the general election which Disraeli called on the issue. 'My mission is to pacify Ireland,' he commented, and the Irish Church Act was passed in 1869. The Church of Ireland, which now became a voluntary body, received substantial compensation for the loss of revenue. Payments were also made to the Presbyterian Church, which lost its *regium donum*, and to the Catholic college at Maynooth, which also lost an annual grant.

In 1870 Gladstone secured the passage of a Land Act aimed at strengthening the position of tenants. It gave the 'Ulster custom', where it existed, the force of law. Elsewhere tenants who gave up their holdings

TO
CHARLES STEWART PARNELL

"NO·MAN·HAS·A·RIGHT·TO·FIX·THE
BOUNDARY·TO·THE·MARCH·OF·A·NATION·
NO·MAN·HAS·A·RIGHT
TO·SAY·TO·HIS·COUNTRY
THUS·FAR·SHALT·THOU
GO·AND·NO·FURTHER·
WE·HAVE·NEVER·
ATTEMPTED·TO·FIX
THE·NE·PLUS·ULTRA
TO·THE·PROGRESS·OF
IRELANDS·NATIONHOOD
AND·WE·NEVER·SHALL"

ᵹo ᴄoιmbιᵹιᴏ᷍ Oιa
éιᴘe ᴅa claιnn

were to receive compensation for improvements they had made, and they were to get a payment for 'disturbance' if they were evicted for any reason other than non-payment of rent. The Act proved a disappointment in practice, for it left too much for the courts to decide, and tenants could not always afford litigation, but at least it indicated that Liberals in Great Britain were willing to attempt reform.

However, Gladstone forfeited the goodwill of the Catholic hierarchy in Ireland when in 1873 he introduced a University Bill which offered no financial assistance to the Catholic University set up in 1854. The hierarchy had opposed the non-denominational Queen's Colleges founded in Belfast, Cork and Galway under an 1845 Act. Gladstone's bill failed, and it was not until the National University of Ireland was established in 1908 that the hierarchy achieved something approximating to its objective of state-aided denominational education at university level.

The Age of Parnell

Two issues dominated the 1870s and 1880s, namely home rule and land reform, and they were often intertwined. Isaac Butt was a barrister, a novelist, and a pamphleteer, writing on land tenure and education matters. The son of a Church of Ireland clergyman, born in 1813 Butt became a barrister. As a Unionist he would speak against Daniel O'Connell, but later defended Fenians in 1865 and campaigned for an amnesty.

Charles Stewart Parnell
Born in County Wicklow in 1846, son of a wealthy Anglo-Irish landowner and an American mother who was descended from Ulster Presbyterians and hated England. Parnell was educated at Cambridge University, owned horses and might have settled into an unthinking life typical of his class, but he was much disturbed by the execution of the Manchester martyrs in 1867, and decided that Ireland needed better government. Elected to parliament in 1875, he adopted obstructionist tactics to force attention to Irish affairs. In 1879 he became president of the Land League, and in 1880 leader of the Irish parliamentary party. He was jailed without trial in 1881-2, but was released when the

Left: Statue to Charles Stewart Parnell

government agreed to reform the land laws. After 1885 Parnell's party held a balance of power at Westminster, and Home Rule for Ireland became a real possibility. In 1887 he survived a series of hostile articles in The Times which proved to be based on forged evidence. In 1889 he was cited in a divorce action brought by the MP husband of Kitty O'Shea, with whom he had lived for many years. His supporters split over the scandal, and in 1890 'The Chief' was voted out of the leadership. No longer the uncrowned king of Ireland, he tried in vain to regain support with a heavy programme of meetings and speeches. He died in 1891.

Having converted to nationalism, the object of Butt's 1870 Home Government Association was to press for an Irish parliament with full control over domestic affairs, envisaging a federal system in which Ireland would continue to send members to the parliament at Westminster. The association was not really a political organisation, but Butt and some other members won by-elections, and disappointment with Gladstone's University Bill led Irish Liberals to adopt the home rule cause. The association was replaced in 1873 by a stronger Home Rule League, and after the 1874 election (the first with a secret ballot) there were fifty-nine MPs committed to home rule. They immediately formed a political party, but Butt was an ineffectual leader, too moderate, too conservative to adopt new tactics which would force Irish problems to Westminster's attention. It was left to Joseph Biggar, a Belfast businessman who had joined the Irish Republican Brotherhood, and a few others to obstruct the business of the Commons by shrewd exploitation of parliamentary rules. The man who welded the Irish parliamentary party into a cohesive force, however, was a southern Protestant landlord named Charles Stewart Parnell.

Parnell was not a natural orator, but he had a handsome and commanding appearance, and his passionate feelings were matched by sound political judgement. He was first elected at a by-election in County Meath in 1875, and two years later replaced Butt as president of the Home Rule Confederation of Great Britain. Butt was a spent force in 1877, and Parnell had won Fenian support by championing the Manchester martyrs in parliament. Two years later Butt was dead. The conservative elements in the party disapproved of Parnell's obstructionist tactics, and not until after the elections of 1880 did Parnell take over leadership of the party.

He had also become president of the newly formed Irish National Land League in October 1879. The Land League was the creation of Michael Davitt. Born in County Mayo in 1846, son of a small farmer who was evicted in 1852 and settled in Lancashire. After losing an arm as a child labourer in a cotton mill he acquired some schooling. In 1865 he joined the Fenian Brotherhood, and took part in a raid on Chester Castle in 1867, for which he was imprisoned 1870-7. In 1879, a year of famine, he organised a large demonstration against a proposed eviction in County Mayo. From 1877 Davitt earned his living as a writer. His best known book is Leaves From a Prison Diary (1884), which proposed a labour party in Britain . The objects of the Land League were to prevent rack-renting (exorbitant rents) and eviction and to make tenants owners of the land they farmed. It quickly brought pressure to bear on anyone who attempted to take over a farm after an eviction, and one of the first victims of this policy of ostracism was a landowner's agent, Captain Charles Boycott, whose name passed into the language. Although the government was eventually forced into legislation by which tenant farmers could buy their land, Davitt continued to argue for land nationalisation. He finally broke with the more conservative Parnell over the latter's divorce case, won a Westminster seat in 1895, but resigned in 1899 over the Boer War. He died of blood poisoning in 1906.

Another figure of importance was John Devoy, one of the leaders of the American Fenian movement, now known as Clan na Gael or the United Brotherhood. Devoy was persuaded of the effectiveness of parliamentary activity on obstructionist lines, and was particularly insistent that land reform should be a principal concern. The Fenian movement gave substantial financial and other support to the parliamentary party and the Land League, and the loose alliance between Devoy, Davitt and Parnell became known as the 'New Departure'.

In 1880 Gladstone regained the premiership. He introduced a bill to protect tenants in arrears against eviction, but it was defeated in the Lords and agrarian disorders increased. In 1881 he produced a Coercion Bill, but followed it with a measure more revolutionary than the one that had failed, and this time the Conservatives in the upper house allowed it to pass. The Land Act guaranteed 'the three Fs', namely fair rent, fixity of tenure, and free sale of the tenancy at market values. However, fixity of tenure depended on the payment of rent, and many tenants were already in arrears. Secondly, while the Act provided for land courts to fix rent by arbitration, there was no clear indication of what would constitute a fair rent. Some of Parnell's supporters were virulently opposed to the new legislation, and he himself spoke so vigorously that in October 1881 he was arrested under the Coercion Act and imprisoned in Kilmainham Jail in Dublin. The Land League was also suppressed, and there was an increase in violence throughout the country. The government realised that Parnell could do more good out of prison, and secret negotiations led to the 'Kilmainham treaty' and his release in May 1882. The government agreed to extend the scope of the Act and to deal with the arrears problem, while Parnell was to discourage violence and intimidation.

His leadership might have been in danger, but four days after his release the new chief secretary of Ireland, Lord Frederick Cavendish, was assassinated in Phoenix Park on his first evening in Dublin, along with his under-secretary, T.H. Burke. The assassins belonged to a secret society known as the Invincibles, and Parnell was so shocked that he considered leaving public life. Gladstone was among those who dissuaded him, and Parnell held the national movement together by his attack on new coercion legislation.

A new organisation, the Irish National League, was formed in 1882, and placed its emphasis on home rule rather than land reform. The land war was in abeyance, and subsequent governments were to pass legislation assisting tenants to buy their farms. Parnell declared that 'No man has a right to fix the boundary of the march of a nation', but he was prepared to accept for Ireland a subordinate parliament dealing with domestic affairs. The election of 1885 gave Parnell a party of eighty-six members, and he held a balance of power between Gladstone's Liberals and Lord Salisbury's Conservatives. Gladstone took office with Parnell's support, and in April 1886 presented his first Home Rule Bill, which provided for an Irish parliament and executive. With ninety-three Liberals voting against the bill it was defeated by 343 votes to 313, and the Conservatives won the subsequent general election.

Parnell was now committed to a Liberal alliance in the hope that it would ultimately lead to home rule. His reputation in Britain was high, and rose further when an article in *The Times* suggested that he had approved of the Phoenix Park murders, for a government commission proved that the incriminating evidence had been forged. However, in December 1889 Parnell was cited as co-respondent in a divorce action brought by an Irish MP, Capt. William O'Shea. He offered no defence and subsequently married Kitty O'Shea, but the scandal cost him the leadership of his party. He died in October 1891 at the age of forty-five, worn out and embittered by his vain attempt to hold on to power. Yet, although he left a party deeply divided between those who had supported him and those who had 'betrayed' him, his reputation survived and endures. Even in his resistance to the efforts of the Irish hierarchy and Gladstone to persuade him to give up the party leadership, he is seen by admirers as rejecting clerical influence in politics and warning of the dangers of alliance with any British party.

'Ulster Will Fight'

Throughout the nineteenth century the Protestants of Ulster had become increasingly committed to the Union with Great Britain. The northern province had suffered fewer religious disabilities, the 'Ulster custom' had produced more prosperous agriculture, the great Famine had bitten less deeply and the industrial revolution produced an economy quite different from the rest of Ireland. Once Catholic emancipation had been granted, the Protestants realised they would be in a minority in any Irish parliament, and sectarian rioting became common as the Orange Order persuaded its followers that Home Rule meant Rome rule.

When Gladstone became prime minister in 1886, a leading Conservative, Lord Randolph Churchill, wrote: 'I decided some time ago that if the G.O.M. [ie, Gladstone, the Grand Old Man] went for Home Rule, the Orange card was the one to play.' Churchill coined the slogan "Ulster will fight, and Ulster will be right" and forged a lasting alliance between the Conservatives and the Ulster Unionists. The riots of 1886 were the worst in Belfast's history, and there was another serious outbreak in 1893, after Gladstone had introduced his second Home Rule Bill, which was defeated in the Lords.

In 1905 the Ulster Unionist Council was formed, linking Unionist associations and the Orange Order. Unionists in the rest of Ireland had the Irish Unionist Alliance, and in Great Britain there was a Union Defence League, but it was apparent that Northern Protestants were prepared to sacrifice their co-religionists in the other provinces to ensure their own place in the United Kingdom. The Liberals regained power in 1905, but before presenting the new Home Rule Bill it was necessary to bring forward legislation curbing the power of the House of Lords. The Unionists continued to organise, and in 1910 the Westminster members chose as their leader Sir Edward Carson, an eminent barrister who represented the University of Dublin. The following year Carson told a

Ireland under the Union

mass rally near Belfast that Unionists must be prepared 'the morning Home Rule passes, ourselves to become responsible for the government of the Protestant province of Ulster'.

Edward Carson

Born in Dublin in 1854, son of an architect of Scottish origin. He studied law at Trinity College, Dublin, where a fellow student was Oscar Wilde, whom he later prosecuted. A fine debater at college, he rose rapidly at the bar, becoming known as 'Coercion Carson' when he assisted the chief secretary, Arthur Balfour, in prosecuting land agitators. In 1892 he became MP for Dublin University so that he could be appointed Irish Solicitor-General, and embarked on a successful legal career in Britain. He was knighted and became British Solicitor-General in 1900. While in opposition he agreed in 1910 to lead the Unionists in their struggle against Home Rule. During World War I Carson served in the war cabinet, and in 1918 was elected MP for the Duncairn division of Belfast. After giving up the Unionist leadership in 1921 he became Lord Carson of Duncairn. He died in 1935.

The Government of Ireland Bill was published in April 1912, and proposed that an Irish parliament should have jurisdiction only over domestic affairs. It was a very limited measure, but the Unionists were encouraged to resist by Bonar Law and other leading Conservatives, and almost half a million signed an Ulster Covenant pledging themselves to 'all means which may be found necessary to defeat the present conspiracy to set up a Home Rule Parliament in Ireland'. Plans were laid for a provisional government.

The Bill was passed by the Commons in January 1913, but the Lords rejected it. However, under the Parliament Act of 1911 the Lords had only power to delay the legislation, and if the government and the Commons remained resolute the Bill would eventually become law. Meanwhile the situation in Ireland deteriorated. In March 1914 a number of army officers at the Curragh camp near Dublin offered their resignations rather than face the possibility of being ordered to act against the Ulster Unionists. The following month a successful gunrunning operation provided arms

Left: Statue of Carson in grounds of Stormont, Belfast

for the Ulster Volunteer Force which the Ulster Unionist Council had set up the previous year. The Liberal prime minister, Herbert Asquith, convened a conference of the conflicting political parties in the hope of reaching a compromise agreement by which a part of Ireland would be excluded from Home Rule, but it failed. In July the Irish Volunteers, a nationalist force set up as a response to the UVF, landed guns at Howth, near Dublin.

In August the situation was completely altered by the outbreak of World War I. John Redmond, leader of the Irish parliamentary party, promised support for Britain's war effort. The Government of Ireland Act reached the statute-book on 18 September 1914, but there was an accompanying provision that it should not come into operation until the war had ended.

The Irish Renaissance

The Irish parliamentary party was so divided and demoralised after Parnell's downfall that for many years it made little political impact. The Conservatives hoped to 'kill Home Rule with kindness', and conciliatory policies were adopted. Land reform continued, Horace Plunkett's co-operative movement helped to improve agricultural practices, and in 1891 a Congested Districts Board was established to amalgamate holdings and improve living conditions in the impoverished western counties. A number of light railways were built to reduce the isolation of these areas.

Yet, if there was a lull in the parliamentary struggle, elsewhere there was an important awakening of national feeling. In 1884 the Gaelic Athletic Association had been formed to preserve and cultivate such native sports as hurling and Gaelic football, and the movement spread rapidly, imposing on its members a separatist outlook which forbade them to play 'foreign games'. In 1893 the Gaelic League was founded by Douglas Hyde, son of a Church of Ireland rector, and Eoin MacNeill. The objective was to revive the Irish language, which had declined because of the National School system and because the Famine had been most severe in Irish-speaking areas. An accompanying movement was the upsurge of Anglo-Irish literature and drama, in which writers like W.B. Yeats, Lady Gregory, James Stephens and Standish O'Grady awakened interest in the legends and folklore of Ireland. The spirit of their works, written in English, was heroic and nationalist and helped to nourish dreams of independence.

The Irish Republican Brotherhood was still in existence, and its members were deeply involved in the Gaelic Athletic Association from the beginning, seeing it as a means of fostering youthful republicanism. It grew in influence after 1898, the year in which the 1798 rising was commemorated, and a Local Government Act in that year created new county councils which revitalised political activity at a local level. However, the most significant political counterpart of the cultural renaissance was the foundation of *Sinn Fein* (Ourselves Alone) in 1905. Its moving spirit was Arthur Griffith. Born in Dublin in 1871, Griffith worked in a printing office before emigrating to Transvaal, where he organised a commemoration of the 1798 rising. He returned to Ireland in 1899 and founded a journal, the *United Irishman*, which called for a complete political and economic separation from Great Britain, arguing that Irish MPs should withdraw from Westminster and form a separate assembly in Dublin. He proposed a dual monarchy of the kind that existed in Hungary, and wanted to make existing British institutions unworkable by setting up Irish ones.

In 1905 he founded the Sinn Fein movement, and sought passive resistance to British rule. Griffith left the Irish Republican Brotherhood in 1906, and was not active in the 1916 rising, but his movement became the political counterpart of physical-force republicanism and soon swept to electoral success. Griffith yielded the presidency of Sinn Fein to de Valera in 1917. During the treaty negotiations of 1921 Griffith led the Irish delegation in London, and in January 1922 he succeeded de Valera as president of Dáil Éireann. In August he died. Griffith's writings had been influential, but this thoughtful and unassuming man left behind an Ireland partitioned and in the midst of a civil war, which he had not sought.

The Easter Rising

Arthur Griffith was not an advocate of physical force, but he began to lose ground to those who were. Tom Clarke, a veteran Fenian, returned from America in 1907 and began to build up the Irish Republican Brotherhood at the expense of Sinn Fein. By 1910 the IRB had its own journal, *Irish Freedom*, and was attracting men like Patrick Pearse and Thomas MacDonagh, who were imbued with the ideals of the Gaelic League. There was an active labour movement led by James Connolly, founder of the Irish Socialist Republican Party, and Jim Larkin. In 1913 a series of strikes was followed by a lockout, and the Irish Citizen Army was formed to protect the strikers from the police. The Irish Volunteers were established under the presidency of Eoin MacNeill in November 1913. Their objectives were not well defined, but MacNeill, now a professor of early Irish history, envisaged a defensive organisation comparable to the eighteenth-century Volunteers, and argued that the UVF in the north was really a Home-Rule movement determined not to let Britain decide Ireland's fate. The IRB saw the Volunteers as a useful weapon, possessing a moderate front but capable of being turned to insurrection, and quickly took over a number of key offices in the movement.

James Connolly

Born in Edinburgh in 1868, of Irish parents. He knew poverty all his life, and worked from the age of eleven before joining the British Army. In 1889 he married and returned to Edinburgh, working as a carter and becoming active in trade unionism. In 1896 he came to Dublin and formed the Irish Socialist Republican Party. He emigrated to America in 1903, becoming an organiser for the Industrial Workers of the World (the Wobblies). He founded the Irish Socialist Federation in New York in 1907. Connolly returned to Ireland in 1910, and helped to organise the dockers and mill girls of Belfast. He joined Jim Larkin in the great Dublin strike of 1913, was jailed and went on hunger strike, and in 1914 formed his trade unionists into the Irish Citizen Army. He commanded the forces which occupied the GPO in Dublin in 1916, and was severely wounded before surrendering. He was executed in a chair, unable to stand before the firing squad. Connolly's writings, notably Labour in Irish History (1910), and his concept of a workers' republic have remained influential.

When war broke out, the IRB leaders saw England's difficulty as Ireland's opportunity and set up a military council, which eventually decided on Easter 1916 as the time for rebellion. Its members were Pearse, Connolly, Clarke, MacDonagh, Sean MacDiarmada, Joseph Plunkett and Eamonn Ceannt, and Pearse, in particular, saw the need for a blood sacrifice which would inspire the Irish people to a final struggle for freedom. However the rising itself was a failure. A German ship carrying arms was captured by a British vessel. MacNeill, who had been kept in the dark, learned of the proposed insurrection two days

Above: Cross marking the execution spot of James Connolly

before it was due to occur, and cancelled Volunteer manoeuvres planned for Easter Sunday. The military council had hoped to use the manoeuvres to launch the rising, but these initial setbacks did not deter them. On Easter Monday an insurgent army occupied a number of public buildings in Dublin, making the General Post Office the headquarters of 'the provisional government of the Irish Republic'. Pearse stood on the steps of the GPO and read out a document, signed by the seven members of the military council, proclaiming the republic.

Patrick Pearse
Born in Dublin in 1879, son of an English stonemason and an Irish mother from County Meath. Patrick (or Padraic) Pearse developed an early preoccupation with Irish history, and in childhood games would cast himself as self-sacrificing martyr. He taught himself Irish, and later had a cottage in Connemara which is now a national monument. On graduating from the Royal University of Ireland he became editor of the Gaelic League's magazine. In 1908 he founded St Enda's School in the suburb of Rathmines, moving in 1910 to larger premises at Rathfarnham. The original building became St Ita's, a school for girls, and in both Irish was the principal language for teaching. Pearse founded his own journal in 1912, and increasingly supported the use of physical force to achieve political ends. He joined the Irish Republican Brotherhood, and as a member of its supreme council planned the 1916 rising. He also became director of organisation of the Irish Volunteers. In 1915 he gave the oration at the funeral of an old Fenian, O'Donovan Rossa, saying: 'Life springs from death; and from the graves of patriot men and women spring living nations.' In 1916 he was chosen to be president of the republicans' provisional government and commandant-general of the army. He proclaimed the Republic at the GPO in Dublin on Easter Monday, and signed the surrender order the following Saturday. He wrote poetry as he waited to be executed.

The republican forces consisted of about 1,300 Volunteers and 200 members of Connolly's Citizen Army, and within a week they had given up the uneven battle. There had been little or no popular support for the rising, but martial law had been imposed and there were widespread arrests. More than ninety people were sentenced to death at courts

Above: A cell in Kilmainham Gaol with an inscription of a poem by Patrick Pearse

martial, and fifteen, including the signatories of the proclamation, were executed before the government gave way to the rising tide of public outrage and called a halt. Later in the year Sir Roger Casement, who had negotiated for assistance from Germany, was hanged in England for treason. A northern Protestant, he had earlier served with distinction in the British consular service.

The War of Independence

Although Sinn Fein as an organisation had not been directly involved in the Easter Rising, it seized the political benefits and defeated the discredited parliamentary party at a number of by-elections in 1917. One of the victors, in East Clare, was Eamon de Valera, the only surviving commandant of the rising, and before the year ended he succeeded Griffith as leader of Sinn Fein. In the general election of December 1918, Sinn Fein won seventy-three Irish seats, the Unionists twenty-six, and the parliamentary party was left with only six members. The Sinn Fein members refused to take their seats at Westminster, and instead met in Dublin in January 1919 as *Dáil Éireann* (Assembly of Ireland). De Valera was in prison at this time because Sinn Fein and the Volunteers had been declared illegal the previous May, but he escaped from Lincoln Jail in February, and was elected president of the Dáil in April. He soon left for America to raise funds and to seek American support for the Irish Republic at the Versailles peace conference.

Michael Collins
Born in West Cork in 1890, son of a farmer who belonged to the Fenian Brotherhood. In 1906 he passed the Post Office entrance examination, and worked in various jobs in London until 1916. He was active in the Gaelic League and the Gaelic Athletic Association, and in 1909 joined the secret Irish Republican Brotherhood. He fought in the GPO in Dublin during the 1916 rising, and was later imprisoned in England and Wales. Collins helped to organise the IRA, and established an intelligence network which penetrated Dublin Castle. When Dáil Éireann met in 1919 he was named Minister of Home Affairs and later de Valera's Minister of Finance. The 'Big Fellow' became a legendary figure during the War of Independence, miraculously eluding capture. In December 1921 he signed the Anglo-Irish Treaty, saying, 'I have signed my own death warrant.' In January 1922 he became chairman of the Provisional Government of the Irish Free State, and in June ordered the attack on the Republican garrison in the Four Courts. He was made commander-in-chief of the Provisional Government's forces in July. On 22 August 1922 he was killed in an ambush in the valley of Beal na mBlath, less than twenty miles from his birthplace.

Ireland slipped steadily into a state of war, in which the Irish Republican Army emerged to conduct a highly successful guerrilla campaign against police and troops. Much of the resistance was directed by Michael Collins, who had fought in the GPO in 1916, and now applied a cool and ruthless intellect to intelligence work. In March 1920 the British government reinforced the Royal Irish Constabulary with ex-soldiers nicknamed 'Black and Tans' because they wore a mixture of police and army uniform. They were joined in August by the Auxiliaries, who were ex-officers. Both forces engaged in atrocities, torturing,

Right: The Four Courts were attacked in 1922 under orders from Michael Collins

burning, and killing in an undisciplined way. The Irish for their part were unmerciful in their treatment of crown forces or suspected informers, and IRA 'flying columns' carried out many successful ambushes. Many of the 'big houses' of the Anglo-Irish gentry were burned down.

The British prime minister, David Lloyd George, sought a compromise settlement in the Government of Ireland Act, which became law in 1920. It provided for parliaments for 'Northern Ireland', consisting of six Ulster counties, and for 'Southern Ireland'. Elections were held in May, and the republican government agreed that Sinn Fein would take part so that the people's will could be demonstrated. The Unionists won forty of the fifty-two seats in the Northern Ireland parliament, and Sir James Craig formed a government, having succeeded the ageing and disappointed Carson. In the twenty-six counties of 'Southern Ireland' Sinn Fein candidates were unopposed in 124 seats, while the remaining four seats went to Unionists representing Dublin University. The Sinn Fein members formed themselves into the second Dáil Éireann. Lloyd George now offered the war-weary republicans a truce, to be followed by tripartite talks involving the British government and the two parts of Ireland. The offer was accepted and the War of Independence ended at noon on 11 July 1921.

The Treaty

The treaty negotiations in London lasted almost five months, and the British delegation under Lloyd George was insistent throughout this period that Ireland should remain part of the British empire and owe allegiance to the crown, and that the six counties of Northern Ireland should not be forced against their will into any new Irish state. The Irish delegation was led by Arthur Griffith, and included Michael Collins. De Valera remained in Dublin. With much misgiving the Irish delegates signed the 'Articles of agreement for a treaty between Great Britain and Ireland' on 6 December 1921, after Lloyd George had threatened an immediate resumption of war. The Anglo-Irish Treaty provided that the new 'Irish Free State' should have dominion status, that members of its parliament should take an oath of allegiance to the crown, and that Britain should maintain naval bases in certain Irish ports. Northern Ireland was given the right to opt out of the Irish Free State, and the parliament in Belfast immediately took advantage of this. There was then provision for a boundary commission to adjust the existing border 'in accordance with the wishes of the inhabitants, so far as may be compatible with economic and geographic conditions'.

The delegates returned to Dublin, and the Dáil cabinet was immediately divided over whether or not to accept the terms of the treaty. De Valera was unwilling to agree to the oath of allegiance, but the signatories believed they had got the best terms possible, and Collins told the Dáil they had achieved 'not the ultimate freedom that all nations aspire and develop to, but the freedom to achieve it'. The partition of the island, which was to prove the most intractable problem, received remarkably little attention in the debate. Collins undoubtedly assumed that the boundary commission would take note of the Catholic majorities in Fermanagh and Tyrone, and that Northern Ireland would be reduced to the four counties of Londonderry, Antrim, Down and Armagh and would not survive as a separate unit. On 7 January 1922 the Dáil voted by sixty-four votes to fifty-seven to accept the treaty. De Valera resigned the presidency, and was succeeded by Griffith. On 16 January a provisional government led by Michael Collins took possession of Dublin Castle, and the evacuation of British troops and administrators began.

Modern Ireland

The Civil War

Ireland drifted steadily towards civil war. The political split over the treaty was paralleled in the IRA, and in March 1922 a convention of dissidents repudiated the Dáil and pledged allegiance to the republic of 1916. In April the 'Irregulars' occupied the Four Courts, the Dublin headquarters of the Irish judiciary, and some other buildings and turned them into fortified points. Collins hoped that a general election might produce a solution, and took no action. It was held on 16 June, and out of 128 seats 58 went to pro-treaty candidates, 36 to anti-treaty republicans led by de Valera, 17 to Labour, and 17 to various other interests. Only the republicans were still unwilling to accept the treaty, and when a party from the Four Courts kidnapped a pro-treaty general later in the month, Collins ordered an attack on the building.

On 28 June Free State troops opened fire with artillery borrowed from the remnant of the British army still in Dublin, and two days later the garrison surrendered. The Civil War had begun, and it was fought with increasing bitterness as the Irregulars employed guerrilla tactics among a population on whose support they could no longer rely. An exhausted Griffith died on 12 August, and Collins was killed in an ambush ten days later. When the new Dáil met in September, William T. Cosgrave was elected president, and Kevin O'Higgins took the important post of Minister of Home Affairs. The republicans refused to recognise the Dáil, and in October set up a rival government under de Valera. A new constitution was approved both by the Dáil and by the Westminster parliament, and on 6 December 1922 the Irish Free State formally came into existence. The government took exceptionally severe steps to deal with the Irregulars, and army courts were empowered to execute anyone found in unauthorised possession of arms or ammunition. When a member of the Dáil was shot dead on 7 December the government ordered four leading republican prisoners to be executed in reprisal the following morning. In April 1923 the Irregulars' chief of staff, Liam Lynch, was killed in action. His successor, Frank Aiken, agreed with de Valera that they could not hope to win the war, and a negotiated truce led to a ceasefire on 24 May.

Reconstruction

The Free State government's most pressing task was to restore respect for law and order. Violence had become a way of life with many people and, although the Civil War was over, the republicans still looked on the government as illegitimate. Increasingly the political stage was dominated by the young Kevin O'Higgins. He modelled himself on Michael Collins, the 'Big Fellow', and while he did not shrink from harsh measures, he never lost sight of the normality which was his objective. One of the most farsighted moves was to set up an unarmed police force, the *Garda Siochana* or Civic Guard, which replaced the paramilitary Royal Irish Constabulary. A new and more decentralised judicial system was established. At the same time O'Higgins used his powers of internment under the Public Safety Act of 1923, and held many of the republicans taken prisoner during and after the Civil War.

In March 1924 an army mutiny was threatened when a group of 'old IRA' veterans (those who had supported the treaty) called for the removal of the Military Council, in which the Irish Republican Brotherhood had become entrenched, and for a suspension of demobilisation. Cosgrave was ill; O'Higgins took control, and quickly appointed the chief of police to command the defence forces. Two members of the government resigned during the crisis, but O'Higgins made the point to the Dáil that 'Those who take the pay and wear the uniform of the state, be they soldiers or police, must be non-political servants of the state', and an inquiry provided an opportunity to put the army on a sounder footing.

The 1920s were constructive years, though marred by the assassination of O'Higgins in July 1927. A new civil service replaced the British administration, and a strong new system of local government was created, with city and county managers on American lines. The Electricity Supply Board, the first of many state-sponsored bodies, was set up in 1927 and undertook an ambitious hydro-electricity scheme on the river Shannon which became a source of national pride. Ireland was quick to join the League of Nations, and within the British Commonwealth asserted the independence of dominions with considerable success at imperial conferences. Cosgrave's party was known as *Cumann na nGaedheal*, becoming *Fine Gael* (Tribe of Gaels) in 1933. In 1926 de Valera broke with the rump of the IRA, resigned from Sinn Fein, and formed a new party called *Fianna Fail* (Warriors of Destiny), which contested the 1927 election. It became the largest opposition party in the Dáil as de Valera and others reluctantly took the oath of allegiance, making it clear that they considered it an empty formula.

Eamon de Valera

Born in New York in 1882, son of an Irish mother and a Spanish father. The latter died in 1885, and the young boy was brought up on the family farm in County Limerick. He became a mathematics teacher, joined the Gaelic League in 1908 and the Irish Volunteers in 1913. During the 1916 rising he commanded one of the four battalions of Volunteers in Dublin, and possibly escaped execution because of his American birth. Released from prison in 1917 he won the East Clare by-election, and became president of Sinn Fein. He was interned in 1918, but escaped from Lincoln Jail a year later and was chosen as president of Dáil Éireann. He opposed the Treaty of 1921, and headed the republicans' 'emergency government' during the Civil War. De Valera finally broke with the IRA, formed the Fianna Fail party, and won the 1932 election. He introduced a new constitution in 1937 and held power almost without interruption until his resignation in 1959, when he was elected President of Ireland, a post to which he was re-elected in 1966. In the twentieth century, only Winston Churchill matched de Valera's political durability, but the Irishman concentrated rather narrowly on Irish problems, although he became president of the League of Nations in 1938. The 1937 constitution reflected a Catholic conservatism which contrasted with his earlier revolutionary activities, and his vision was of an unmaterialistic Gaelic-speaking Ireland. He retired from office in 1973, and died in 1975.

Meanwhile the existing border between Northern Ireland and the Irish Free State had been confirmed. The three-man boundary commission had interpreted its terms of reference very narrowly, and in November 1925 a report in the London *Morning Post* indicated that only minor changes would be recommended, and that these would include transferring part of Donegal to Northern Ireland. Eoin MacNeill, the Irish member, resigned from the commission and later from the cabinet. There was a hasty meeting of representatives of the British, Irish and Northern

Right: Government buildings, Dublin. De Valera's seat of power

Irish governments, and a tripartite agreement was signed in London on 3 December 1925. The powers of the boundary commission were revoked, and Northern Ireland remained the six counties of the 1920 Government of Ireland Act. Not surprisingly de Valera criticised this acceptance of partition as a consequence of the 1921 treaty, and he embarked on the course which was to bring him to power through the ballot-box.

Fianna Fail

One of the last achievements of the Cosgrave administration was the 1931 Statute of Westminster, by which Britain agreed that a dominion parliament could repeal or amend any British Act 'in so far as the same is part of the law of the Dominion'. By this time the government had lost popularity as a result of the economic decline, and it had been forced to introduce repressive measures in response to increasing crimes of violence and the intimidation of juries. The Public Safety Act of 1931 extended police powers of arrest and detention, and set up a military tribunal to try crimes of a political nature. Under the Act a dozen organisations were immediately declared illegal, including the IRA and a breakaway socialist movement, Saor Éire (Free Ireland). In the election of 1932 Fianna Fail won 72 out of 153 seats, becoming the largest party, and with Labour support de Valera formed a government. During the next forty years Fianna Fail was out of office only for two short periods: 1948-51 and 1954-7.

Among Fianna Fail supporters there were some fears that Cumann na nGaedheal might resist a change in government, and at first the Fianna Fail members entered the Dáil with revolvers in their pockets. However, the handover was accomplished peacefully, and de Valera in turn showed respect for those who had laboured to develop the new institutions of the Free State. He quickly abolished the oath of allegiance, and in other ways loosened the ties with the United Kingdom. Sean Lemass, the Minister for Industry and Commerce, pursued a protectionist policy which encouraged Irish industry to develop in an unprecedented way, and in key areas the government set up state-sponsored bodies such as Coras Iompair Éireann (road and rail transport), Aer Lingus (air transport), and Bord na Móna (peat production). When de Valera withheld from the United Kingdom the annuity payments which stemmed from earlier loans to tenants to buy their holdings, the British government retaliated by imposing heavy duties on Irish goods. The economic war lasted until 1938, when the Free State paid £10 million to settle the annuities dispute, and at the same time Britain handed back the treaty ports occupied by the Royal Navy under the 1921 treaty.

Within a few days of taking office in 1932 the government had released IRA prisoners convicted by the military tribunal, and the IRA ceased to be an illegal organisation. The advocates of physical force immediately began military drilling, and freedom of speech was endangered as republicans began to break up meetings of Cumann na nGaedheal. When the commissioner of police, General Eoin O'Duffy, was dismissed, he became leader of the Army Comrades Association, which was renamed the National Guard and known from its uniform as the Blueshirts.

The Blueshirts were defensive in origin, but when O'Duffy announced a mass march in August 1934 to commemorate the deaths of Griffith, Collins and O'Higgins, the government feared a *coup d'état* comparable to Mussolini's march on Rome. The government revived the emergency powers of the Cosgrave era, and banned the march. The military tribunal was restored, and the National Guard was declared illegal. O'Duffy then became president of the newly created Fine Gael party, but his venture into party politics was a failure, and he was succeeded by Cosgrave. In 1936, when the Spanish Civil War broke out, O'Duffy formed an Irish brigade which fought for General Franco.

The IRA always presented de Valera with more serious problems than this Blueshirt flirtation with fascism, and in June 1936 it was again declared an illegal organisation. Its chief of staff, Maurice Twomey, was jailed by the military tribunal soon afterwards, and the movement went underground. In 1939 the IRA launched a campaign of bombing in England, and in one incident in Coventry five people were killed. The Irish government took further measures against those who still proclaimed their loyalty to the republic of 1916, but the IRA was to remain a source of recurring violence.

There had been a number of changes to the 1922 constitution before Fianna Fail came to power, but these were concerned principally to make government more effective. De Valera, in contrast, concentrated on amending provisions which were offensive to his feelings as an Irishman. As well as the oath of allegiance he ended the office of governor-general and abolished the Senate, which had been designed in part as a gesture of friendship towards the unionists of the twenty-six counties. In 1937 he produced a new constitution, *Bunreacht na* hÉireann, which was endorsed at a referendum. Fianna Fail won exactly half the Dáil seats at the election held on the same day. The constitution was an unusual document, reflecting republican ideas in its reference to a 'sovereign, independent, democratic state' deriving all powers of government from the people, and at the same time acknowledging God as the ultimate source of all authority and basing many of its articles on contemporary Catholic social theory.

The new constitution provided for a two-chamber parliament or Oireachtas, with an elected president or Uachtarán as head of state and a system of cabinet government headed by a prime minister or Taoiseach. The national territory was defined to include the thirty-two counties of Ireland, but pending 're-integration' the jurisdiction of parliament was restricted to twenty-six counties. The state was named as 'Eire, or in the English language, Ireland'. The constitution recognised the special position of the Roman Catholic Church as 'the guardian of the Faith professed by the great majority of the citizens', but recognised other churches then in existence and guaranteed freedom of conscience and religion 'subject to public order and morality'. The family was recognised as 'the natural primary and fundamental unit group of Society' and divorce was forbidden.

Douglas Hyde

Born in 1860, son of a rector in County Roscommon. He grew up in an Irish-speaking district and soon learned the songs and stories of the countryside. A gold medallist at Trinity College, Dublin, Hyde first thought to enter the ministry, but decided instead to make the Irish language his life's work. He published his first collection of folk tales in 1889, and a succession of books in Irish and English established him as a poet and scholar. In 1908 he was appointed to the chair of Modern Irish in the new National University in Dublin. In 1893 he founded the Gaelic League to encourage interest in the language and in Irish music and sports, hoping that the League would provide a meeting ground where nationalist and unionist could share their love of Ireland. However, Sinn Fein's influence became strong, and in 1915 he resigned the presidency after the annual conference committed itself to 'working for a free Ireland'. Hyde enjoyed widespread respect and, after becoming a senator in 1925, he was elected unopposed as president of Ireland under the 1937 constitution. He served from 1938 until 1945, and died in 1949.

When World War II broke out in September 1939 the Free State remained neutral. The British government considered pressing for naval facilities at the former treaty ports, and possibly occupying them by force if necessary, but the existence of a important naval base at Londonderry allowed Britain to safeguard its western approaches without infringing Free State territory. Later the Americans considered the seizure of bases in southern Ireland, in part because they were concerned that information about the coming invasion of Europe might be passed to Germany, which had an ambassador in Dublin. However, Ireland never became of sufficient strategic importance that an invasion was attempted by any of the combatants, and the IRA's contacts with Germany had little practical effect on the war or the Irish situation. De Valera for his part refused to act on an ill defined suggestion from the British prime minister, Winston Churchill, that if the Free State joined the Allies in the war against Germany, it could lead to a united Ireland.

The Republic of Ireland

With the ending of the 'Emergency', as the war was called, the public was ready for a change of government. A radical republican party called *Clann na Poblachta* (Republican Family) emerged under Sean MacBride, and had some success at by-elections. De Valera called a general election in February 1948, and although Fianna Fail remained easily the largest party, a variety of other parties united to form an uneasy coalition with Fine Gael's John A. Costello as Taoiseach. Before the year ended, the Republic of Ireland Act has been passed, declaring Ireland a republic and taking it out of the British Commonwealth. The Republic was formally inaugurated in Easter Monday, 1949. In the same year Westminster passed the Ireland Act, which affirmed that 'in no event will Northern Ireland or any part thereof cease to be part of His Majesty's dominions and of the United Kingdom without the consent of the Parliament of Northern Ireland'. Traditionally Fine Gael had been more sympathetic than Fianna Fail to retaining links with Britain, but Costello was under pressure from MacBride, and also hoped that meeting demands for a republic might help to take the gun out of Irish politics. In fact the Act made little practical difference to relations with Britain, for the Republic continued to enjoy imperial preference in trading, and Irish citizens living and working in Britain were treated as if they were British citizens. Nor did it make much difference within the twenty-six counties for, although Fianna Fail supported the legislation, de Valera pointed out that in 1916 he had been fighting for an all-Ireland Republic, and he pointedly took no part in the inaugural ceremony.

The inter-party government broke up in 1951, following a controversy over the so-called 'Mother and Child Scheme' proposed by the Minister for Health, Dr Noel Browne, who was a member of Clann na Poblachta. Browne wanted free medical treatment for expectant mothers and for children up to the age of sixteen, but the Catholic hierarchy objected to the scheme as interfering with the rights of the family and the individual, and MacBride called on Browne to resign. The second inter-party government lasted from 1954 to 1957, and ended when Clann na Poblachata withdrew its support because of the government's ineffective economic policies and because it had no positive policy for the unification of Ireland. By this time the IRA was active again, raiding targets in Northern Ireland, and the government had begun to take legal action on a modest scale. In the election of 1957 de Valera gained an overall majority and began to intern IRA suspects, while Clann na Poblachta was almost wiped out. In 1959 de Valera was elected to the presidency, and Sean Lemass became Taoiseach.

Lemass had fought in the GPO building in 1916 and was almost sixty, but he had done much to foster industry and he proved a forward-looking leader more concerned with economic growth than with old mythologies. The IRA campaign ended in 1962, and in 1965 Lemass travelled to Belfast to meet the Northern prime minister, Captain Terence O'Neill, awakening hopes of a better relationship between the two parts of Ireland. It was the first time two Irish prime ministers had met since the 1920s. A new trade agreement with the United Kingdom was concluded in 1965. The country became more outward-looking as Irish soldiers served abroad for the first time with United Nations forces. In 1966 Jack Lynch succeeded Lemass, and pursued similar policies, although his task was made more difficult by the outbreak of sectarian violence between the Protestant and Catholic populations of Northern Ireland and by the resurgence of the IRA. In 1972 Ireland's application for membership of the European Economic Community was accepted with effect from 1 January 1973, and in a referendum the electorate endorsed the move by a five-to-one majority.

The Northern Ireland 'Troubles' increasingly impinged on the Republic, and in 1976 a state of emergency was declared after the IRA assassinated the British Ambassador, Christopher Ewart-Biggs, in

Dublin. In 1979, Earl Mountbatten, a kinsman of Queen Elizabeth II, was murdered near his summer home in County Sligo. Acts of terrorism were much less common than in Northern Ireland, but they encouraged a new climate of criminality in which bank robberies, kidnapping and drug peddling became common. Anglo-Irish relations fluctuated in their cordiality, and in 1982 the Republic withdrew from EEC sanctions against Argentina during the latter's conflict with Britain in the Falkland Islands. In 1983-4, representatives of the three main Irish parties and the northern nationalist Social Democratic and Labour Party (SDLP) met in Dublin as the New Ireland Forum, and made proposals for achieving Irish unity with unionist consent. The governments in Dublin and London also recognised formally the 'unique relationship' between the two islands, and in 1985 an Anglo-Irish Agreement was signed by the Irish and British prime ministers, Garret FitzGerald and Margaret Thatcher. It provided for an inter-governmental conference covering political, legal and security matters and the promotion of cross-border co-operation, with the two governments pledged to work for the accommodation of the 'two traditions' in Northern Ireland.

The 'Troubles' had initiated a period of introspection, in which the Republic forced itself to consider what sort of country it hoped to persuade northern Protestants to join. Controversies over family planning law, over a 1983 constitutional amendment directed against abortion, and over the possible legalisation of divorce, exposed divisions between the churches, between the generations, and between city and rural hinterland, and relations between the government and the Roman Catholic Church came under examination much as in the 1951 'Mother and Child' debate. Moreover, successive Fianna Fail and Fine Gael-Labour governments, faced with a very youthful population, failed to solve pressing problems of inflation and rising unemployment. In 1985, the formation of a Progressive Democratic Party, rejecting Civil War loyalties and advocating a new mixture of economic conservatism and progressive social reforms, foreshadowed a new era of Irish politics.

Northern Ireland

When George V opened the first Northern Ireland parliament in June 1921 he appealed 'to all Irishmen to pause, to stretch out the hand of forbearance and conciliation, to forgive and forget, and to join in making

Above: Stormont, the seat of Northern Irish Government at times of Devolution

for the land they love a new era of peace, contentment and conciliation'. It was a vain hope, and the years of 'Home Rule' in Northern Ireland were marked by recurring violence and a failure to dispel the tensions and differences between the Protestant two-thirds of the population and the Catholic one-third. With slogans like 'Not an inch' and 'No surrender' the Protestants were defensive in outlook, and used the local parliament they had not sought to buttress their ascendancy. The Catholics for their part resented what they considered to be an unnatural and immoral partition of the island, and were reluctant to participate in the public institutions of a regime which they hoped would not survive.

Sectarian violence continued until the end of 1922, and the government took coercive measures, most notably the Special Powers Acts of 1922-33. The new Royal Ulster Constabulary was supplemented by the auxiliary Ulster Special Constabulary, entirely or almost entirely Protestant, which Catholics learned to hate. In 1922 the Unionists abolished proportional representation in local government and re-drew boundaries so as to gain control of a number of councils, including the city of Londonderry, which the Nationalists had formerly held. Proportional representation was abolished in parliamentary elections in 1929, and single-member constituencies replaced multi-member constituencies, but the political balance in parliament was little affected except that both the Unionists and the Nationalists became less vulnerable to splinter groups. Rioting occurred more than once in the 1930s, and in 1935 was particularly serious after the government had banned parades but then withdrew to allow the traditional Orange celebrations in July.

The original intention of the 1920 Government of Ireland Act had been that Northern Ireland would be self-financing, but this soon proved impractical in a period of Depression, and ways were found to subsidise government expenditure from the British exchequer so that 'parity' of social standards and services should be maintained between Northern Ireland and the rest of the United Kingdom. Northern Ireland contributed significantly to the British war effort, although it was not thought advisable to introduce conscription, and afterwards so benefited from the development of Britain's welfare state that living standards were patently higher than in the Republic. The Unionists had no difficulty in maintaining a handsome majority in the parliament at Stormont, on the outskirts of Belfast, and Protestant unity was fostered by such events as the anti-partition campaign launched when the Republic of Ireland was declared and the IRA campaign of 1956-62. The premiership of Sir James Craig, later Lord Craigavon, lasted until his death in 1940. Craig was born in County Down in 1871, son of a millionaire whiskey distiller. After a brief business career he served in the Boer War, where he was briefly captured. He became Unionist MP for East Down in 1906. In 1911 he organised a massive demonstration of Orange Lodges and Unionist clubs at his house, Craigavon, after which plans were laid for a provisional government of Ulster. Capt. Craig's meticulous organisation and Northern obstinacy complemented Carson's more dramatic qualities. He became chief political organiser of the resistance to Home Rule. As Sir James Craig he became Northern Ireland's first prime minister in 1921, and presided over a Unionist government until his death in 1940. He was created Viscount Craigavon in 1927.

He was succeeded by J.M. Andrews, a member of his first cabinet, but there was dissatisfaction with his organisation of the war effort, and in 1943 Sir Basil Brooke, later Lord Brookeborough, took over and held office until 1963.

Brookeborough was succeeded by Capt. Terence O'Neill, a man untrammelled by memories of the 1920s, and the new prime minister began to draw the Catholic population more into the mainstream of Ulster life. His efforts to 'build bridges' drew criticism from those Protestants who distrusted the Catholic community and feared that a rising Catholic population would eventually vote Northern Ireland into the Republic. O'Neill's most outspoken opponent was Rev Ian Paisley, moderator of the small Free Presbyterian church, but within his own party there was much opposition to the 1965 meeting with Sean Lemass. The emergence of a predominantly Catholic civil rights movement in the late 1960s left O'Neill trying to hold a precarious middle position, and after the banning of a civil rights march in Londonderry led to violence in the city on 5 October 1968, he was faced with increasing disorder which led to his resignation in April 1969.

O'Neill's successor, Major James Chichester-Clark, was no more successful in curbing violence. A Protestant march commemorating the siege of Londonderry was attacked in the city in August 1969, and a virtual siege of the nearby Catholic Bogside area was followed by violence in other parts of Northern Ireland. In Belfast Protestants invaded Catholic areas, and the British army was eventually called in to prevent further sectarian conflict. Discussions between the British and Northern Ireland governments led to a series of reforms aimed at tackling the underlying causes of religious conflict in Northern Ireland, but the situation worsened as the IRA – split between the so-called 'Officials' influenced by Marxist ideas and the breakaway 'Provisionals', who were more traditional advocates of violence – saw an opportunity of bringing down the Stormont regime.

The IRA established themselves as 'defenders' of the Catholic districts of Belfast and Londonderry, and these districts became steadily more hostile to the army. A substantial 'no-go' area was created in Londonderry, where police and army could not enter, and in parts of Belfast law enforcement was at a minimum. Chichester-Clark resigned in March 1971, dissatisfied with the British government's unwillingness to intensify the battle against the IRA, and was succeeded by Brian Faulkner, who attempted to involve the Opposition parties in the process of government. However, they largely withdrew from Stormont after the death of two Londonderry youths shot by the army during rioting in July. The decision to withdraw was reinforced when, in August, the British government agreed to Faulkner's proposal to introduce internment. The operation was far from successful, for the level of violence immediately rose as the IRA intensified a bombing campaign directed mainly at commercial premises, and the Catholic population as a whole was alienated. Eventually, in March 1972, the British government decided to suspend the Stormont parliament and government for a year, and a Conservative minister, William Whitelaw, was appointed Secretary of State for Northern Ireland. The hope was that, with the Unionists out of power, conciliatory policies would persuade battle-weary Catholics to reject the IRA and that the threatened 'backlash' of disgruntled Protestants could be avoided.

However, IRA violence continued, and although the British army and the police eventually re-entered the 'no-go' areas, there was an upsurge of militancy among Protestants who distrusted the British government. The government produced proposals for a new Northern Ireland Assembly, in which Protestants and Catholics would share more limited powers than the Stormont parliament had possessed. An election was held in June 1973, using proportional representation, and Whitelaw then negotiated the formation of a coalition administration led by Faulkner and drawn from the Unionists, the SDLP and the moderate Alliance Party. In December 1973, representatives of the British and Irish governments and the new executive met at Sunningdale, in England, and agreed on the formation of a Council of Ireland. The SDLP had insisted on this 'Irish dimension', but the Protestant community as a whole rejected it. The power-sharing executive took office on 1 January 1974, but its authority was fatally undermined by the British general election in February, when anti-Sunningdale candidates took eleven of the twelve Ulster seats, and it collapsed in May in the face of a Protestant workers' strike.

Successive Northern Ireland secretaries sought ways to devolve power to a locally elected administration commanding widespread support among both Protestants and Catholics, but without success. In 1976, the British Government rejected the proposals of a Constitutional Convention dominated by the unionists; an Assembly elected in 1982 came no nearer to the gradual or 'rolling' devolution envisaged at its formation. Levels of violence fluctuated, with the IRA increasingly concentrating its attacks on the security forces. There was also occasional terrorism in Great Britain, as in the murder of the Conservative MP, Airey Neave, in 1979, and the bomb explosion at the Conservative conference at Brighton in 1984. Within Northern Ireland, the strength of the RUC was steadily increased, and the army's role was deliberately diminished; trial without jury was introduced for terrorist offences, but internment ended in 1975.

A recurring problem was republican prisoners' demands for special treatment as 'political prisoners', and in 1981 ten died during a hunger strike, including one who had been elected to Westminster in a by-election. The Provisional IRA's political wing, Sinn Fein, had some success in elections, posing a threat to the SDLP's dominance in the Catholic community. The Anglo-Irish Agreement in 1985 was in part an attempt to bolster constitutional nationalism, but the Unionist Party and Paisley's Democratic Unionist Party reacted angrily, representing the Republic's consultative role as a diminution of British sovereignty and a step towards a united Ireland. Unionist MPs forced by-elections in fifteen seats to demonstrate Protestant hostility to the agreement, and embarked on a policy of non co-operation to frustrate the Agreement. A long-term solution to Northern Ireland's problems seemed as elusive as ever.

Epilogue

So much has happened since the last edition was published in 1986 that it has been necessary to update the author's original text.

The IRA bombed a Remembrance Day service in Enniskillen 1987. Condemnation of the bombing led to an IRA statement of 'deep regret'. Inter-governmental discussions on the problems of Northern Ireland continued. British, Irish and American politicians were involved throughout the late 1990s in behind-the-scenes negotiations.

Following a series of secret talks John Hume of the SDLP and Gerry Adams of Sinn Fein issued a statement in September 1993 on 'creation of a peace process'. The IRA planted a bomb on the Shankill Road in October of that year. In the Downing Street Declaration of December 1993 Prime Minister John Major and Taoiseach Albert Reynolds stated that Britain had no 'selfish strategic or economic interest in Northern Ireland', and would encourage agreement on a political settlement in Ireland, based on the wishes of the people. American President Bill Clinton's visit to Belfast in November 1995 drew more attention to the 'peace process'.

The Mitchell Report of January 1996 set out principles which would lead to all-party talks in Northern Ireland. Chief among the principles were discussion and non-violence, to 'take the gun out of Irish politics'.

The 'Good Friday Agreement' of 1998 resulted in the formation of a power-sharing Northern Ireland Assembly, where non-security matters were decided by local politicians. Both John Hume (SDLP) and David Trimble (UUP) were awarded the Nobel Peace Prize in this year: Trimble went on to become First Minister in the Assembly, with Hume's colleague Seamus Mallon as his Deputy. As part of the Agreement, some people convicted of terrorist acts were released early from prison.

Assembly elections returned Members from both emerging loyalist political and smaller traditional parties. Sinn Fein and the Democratic Unionist Party increased their representation in both Northern Ireland and British politics from the late 1990s to date, gaining seats at the expense of both the SDLP and UUP. Decommissioning of weapons was an element of the agreement, and was the subject of continued discussion and suspicion. The Assembly would subsequently be suspended on a number of occasions due to disputes within and outside the chamber. The Assembly was suspended in 2002, with no sign of resumption.

While governments local and national debated futures, violence continued. Ceasefires and 'cessations' were greeted with apprehension. The IRA ceasefire of 1994 was short-lived, with another declared in 1997. Loyalist paramilitaries in turn declared a ceasefire in 1994. The Real IRA bombing of Omagh in 1998 may be seen as the last major terrorist act of the 'Troubles'. In September 2005 the IRA declared 'arms beyond use'.

Important Dates

432	St Patrick's mission to Ireland
563	St Columcille founds monastery at Iona
590	St Columbanus sails to France
c650	*Book of Durrow*
795	First Viking raids on Ireland
c800	*Book of Kells*
841	Dublin founded by Vikings
1002	Brian Boru acknowledged High King
1014	Brian killed as he defeats Norsemen at Clontarf
1066	*Battle of Hastings: William of Normandy becomes King of England*
1152	Synod of Kells
1169	Norman invasion of Ireland begins
1171	Henry II lands at Waterford
1175	Treaty of Windsor
1215	*Magna Carta signed by King John of England*
1315-18	Bruce invasion
1318	Battle of Faughart: Edward Bruce killed
1366	Statutes of Kilkenny
1394-5	First visit of Richard II
1399	Second visit of Richard II
1455	*Wars of the Roses begin in England*
1477-1513	Rule of Garret More, the Great Earl of Kildare
1492	*Columbus sails to America*
1494-5	Poynings' parliament
1534	Rebellion of Silken Thomas
1541	Irish parliament confirms Henry VIII as King of Ireland
1569-73	First Desmond rebellion
1579-83	Second Desmond rebellion
1586	Plantation of Munster
1588	*Defeat of Spanish Armada*
1591	Foundation of Trinity College, Dublin
1594	Rebellion of Hugh O'Neill, Earl of Tyrone
1598	Battle of the Yellow Ford
1601	Battle of Kinsale: O'Neill defeated
1603	Treaty of Mellifont

1607	Flight of the Earls
1609	Plantation of Ulster
1618-48	*Thirty Years' War in Europe*
1633-40	Sir Thomas Wentworth Lord Deputy
1641	Ulster rising begins
1642	*Civil War begins in England*
1642	Confederation of Kilkenny formed
1646	Battle of Benburb
1649	*Charles I executed*
1649	Oliver Cromwell captures Drogheda and Wexford
1652	Land confiscation begins
1660	*Charles II restored to throne*
1681	Oliver Plunkett executed in London
1689	Siege of Londonderry
1690	William III wins Battle of the Boyne
1691	Treaty of Limerick, followed by land confiscation
1695	Beginning of Penal Laws against Catholics
1720	Act declares British parliament's right to legislate for Ireland
1724	Jonathan Swift's *Drapier's Letters*
1776	*American Declaration of Independence*
1779	Volunteers parade in Dublin: trade restrictions repealed
1782	Convention of Volunteers at Dungannon: Irish parliamentary independence conceded
1789	*French Revolution begins*
1791	Society of United Irishmen formed
1792-3	Catholic Relief Acts ease Penal Laws
1795	Orange Order founded in County Armagh
1798	United Irishmen's rising fails: Wolfe Tone commits suicide
1800	Acts of Union passed: end of Grattan's Parliament
1801	Union of Great Britain and Ireland begins
1803	Robert Emmet's rising fails
1815	*Battle of Waterloo*
1823	Daniel O'Connell forms Catholic Association
1828	O'Connell wins Clare by-election
1829	Catholic emancipation attained
1831	National education system established

1832	*Great Reform Act at Westminster*
1837	*Queen Victoria's reign begins*
1840	O'Connell forms National Repeal Association
1842	Thomas Davis founds the *Nation*
1843	Repeal meeting at Clontarf banned
1845-9	Potato famine causes death, hardship, emigration
1848	Young Irelanders' rising fails
1854	*Crimean War begins*
1858	Fenian movement founded
1861-5	*American Civil War*
1867	Fenian rising fails: 'Manchester martyrs' executed
1869	Church of Ireland disestablished
1870	Gladstone's first Land Act: Isaac Butt forms Home Government Association
1873	Home Rule League formed
1879	Michael Davitt forms Irish National Land League: Land war begins
1880	Charles Stewart Parnell elected leader of Irish parliamentary party
1881	Gladstone's second Land Act: Parnell imprisoned
1882	Lord Frederick Cavendish assassinated in Dublin
1884	Gaelic Athletic Association founded
1886	Gladstone's first Home Rule Bill defeated: rioting in Belfast
1889	Parnell cited in divorce case
1891	Death of Parnell
1893	Gladstone's second Home Rule Bill defeated: more rioting in Belfast: Gaelic League founded
1899	Irish Literary Theatre founded
1904	Abbey Theatre opened
1905	Arthur Griffith founds Sinn Fein movement: Ulster Unionist Council formed to fight Home Rule
1912	Ulster Covenant signed
1913	Formation of Ulster Volunteer Force, Irish Citizen Army and Irish Volunteers
1914	Curragh 'mutiny': gun-running by UVF and Irish Volunteers: Government of Ireland Act suspended after receiving royal assent

1914-18	*World War I*
1916	Easter Rising fails: its leaders executed
1917	*Russian Revolution*
1918	Sinn Fein wins majority of Irish seats at Westminster
1919	First Dáil Éireann meets in Dublin, Eamon de Valera later becoming president: War of Independence begins
1920	Government of Ireland Act provides for separate parliaments in Northern and Southern Ireland
1921	Truce followed by Anglo-Irish Treaty
1922	Treaty approved by Dáil Éireann: establishment of Irish Free State followed by Civil War
1923	Civil War ends
1925	Report of boundary commission remains unpublished: tripartite agreement confirms existing border between Northern Ireland and Irish Free State
1927	De Valera and Fianna Fail party enter Dáil
1932	De Valera gains power
1937	New constitution for Irish Free State
1939-45	Irish Free State remains neutral during World War II
1949	Republic of Ireland inaugurated
1956-62	IRA campaign in Northern Ireland
1965	Prime ministers Sean Lemass and Terence O'Neill meet in attempt to improve North-South relations
1968	Civil rights march in Londonderry banned: sectarian disturbances in Northern Ireland become increasingly serious
1969	British troops called in to maintain peace in Northern Ireland
1970	IRA begins campaign of violence in North
1972	Bloody Sunday (30th January) Ireland becomes a member of the European Economic Community
1985	Anglo-Irish Agreement signed

Post Anglo-Irish Agreement

1987	Enniskillen bombing by IRA
1994	IRA ceasefire. Loyalist paramilitaries ceasefire
1996	IRA ceasefire ends
1997	IRA declare ceasefire
	Northern Ireland-born Mary McAleese succeeds Mary Robinson as Irish President
1998	Good Friday Agreement signed
	Omagh bombed by Real IRA
1999	David Trimble and John Hume win Nobel Peace Prize
2002	Euro becomes sole currency of Republic of Ireland
2005	IRA declare arms 'beyond use'

Further Reading

Beckett, J.C., *A Short History of Ireland* (6th ed., 1979)
Beckett, J.C., *The Making of Modern Ireland* (2nd ed., 1981)
Curtis, Edmund, *A Short History of Ireland* (6th ed., 1950)
Edwards, R. Dudley, *A New History of Ireland* (1972)
Kee, Robert, *The Green Flag* (1972)
Lyons, F.S.L., *Ireland since the Famine* (2nd ed., 1985)
Moody, T.W. and Martin, F.X., *The Course of Irish History* (2nd ed., 1984)

In addition to these general works there are a number of excellent books covering more limited periods of history. These include the eleven-volume *Gill History of Ireland* and the ten-volume *Helicon History of Ireland*, both of which embody much recent research, and several collections of Thomas Davis Lectures originally broadcast by Radio Telefis Eireann.

The latter include:

MacManus, Francis (ed.), *The Years of the Great Test, 1926-39* (1967)
Nowlan, Kevin B. and Williams, T. Desmond (eds), *Ireland in the War Years and After, 1939-51* (1969)
O'Brien, Conor Cruise (ed.), *The Shaping of Modern Ireland* (covering the period 1891-1916) (1960)
Williams, Desmond (ed.), *The Irish Struggle, 1916-1926* (1966)

Most of the major historical figure have attracted biographers, but the quality of writing varies enormously, and too many works are patriotic tracts rather than serious pieces of historical research. However, the level of writing about Irish history has risen substantially in recent years.

The Republic's Department of Foreign Affairs has produced a useful booklet, *Facts About Ireland* (6th ed., 1985), and two valuable guides to history on the ground are:

Harbinson, Peter, *Guide to the National Monuments of Ireland* (2nd ed., 1975)
Killanin, Lord and Duignan, Michael V., *The Shell Guide to Ireland* (2nd ed., 1967)

Acknowledgements

The publishers wish to thank the following for permission to reproduce work in copyright:

© istockphoto.com/Paul Baleta (p 8)
© Constance Kwinn (p 10)
© Northern Ireland Tourist Board (p 12)
© Kelly and Caroline Redeker (pp 14 and 20)
© David Decharte (p 18)
© Stockbyte (pp 24, 34, 36, 52, 78, 99, 105)
© Naomi Corrigan (p 26)
© John Murphy (pp 28, 68, 112)
© istockphoto.com/Ronald Carlucci (p 30)
© Damien Clarke (p 45)
© Yoshika Tabata (p 49)
© Michael Lee Martin (p 56)
© Alan Turner (p 60)
© The National Trust. Photograph by Roger Kinkead. (p 64)
© Dave Bushe (p 67)
© John Cumisky (p 70)
© Ronan Shortall (p 74)
© Bill Holland (p 80)
© Andrea Pflug (p 84)
© Kieran O'Shaughnessy (p 90)
© Zakcq Lockrem (p 95)
© Charlotte Jones (p 97)

Other books by Appletree Press:

Birds of Ireland
Gordon D'Arcy

Ireland possesses an astonishing variety of bird-life, not only in the countryside and on the coast, but also in the town, city centres and suburbs. This guide describes over 120 of the most widespread species. Each is delightfully illustrated in full colour and is accompanied by a description of its distinctive habits. An informative and attractive guide for every bird-lover or anyone interested in learning more about the Irish countryside. Contains a concise description of each species, details of how to spot them and an attractive illustration to make identification easier.

ISBN-10: 0-86281-957-1
ISBN-13: 978-0-86281-957-6

Fish of Ireland
Ian Hill

Ireland is one of the most popular fishing destinations in the world and when you see the vast array of fish available on her coastline and riversides it is easy to understand why people come from all over the world to fish here. This useful guide tells you how to identify the different types of fish, the best places to catch them, what to use and even more importantly how to cook them once you have caught them! Contains attractive illustrations for easy identification.

ISBN-10: 0-86281-958-X
ISBN-13: 978-0-86281-958-3

Irish First Names
Ronan Coghlan

Ronan Coghlan provides a comprehensive dictionary of Irish first names, giving the derivation and history of each name and, where available, the Irish translation. Earlier names now no longer in use are included for historical interest as is advice on choosing a name. Since names reflect a country's past, this book will appeal not only to parents searching for an attractive name but also anyone with a general interest in Irish history.

ISBN-10: 0-86281-962-8
ISBN-13: 978-0-86281-962-0

Irish Phrase Book
Paul Dorris

This convenient guide contains over 1,000 useful words and phrases in Irish and English. Included are chapters on travel and accommodation, sightseeing and shopping, and recreation and sport. In addition there are guidelines on pronunciation, dialect and usage plus a basic grammar. In short, the phrasebook will be ideal for those coming to the language for the first time.

ISBN-10: 0-86281-960-1
ISBN-13: 978-0-86281-960-6